MISES MADE EASIER

Mises Made Easier

A GLOSSARY
FOR
Ludwig von Mises' HUMAN ACTION

Prepared by

Percy L. Greaves, Jr.

With a Foreword by Mrs. Ludwig von Mises

Second edition

FREE MARKET BOOKS

Second printing 1997
ISBN 0-930902-29-7 (cloth)
ISBN 0-930902-30-0 (paper)

Free Market Books
P. O. Box 186
Irvington, NY 10533

About the author: Percy L. Greaves, Jr. (1906–1984), a *magna cum laude* graduate of Syracuse University in business (1929), did graduate work in economics at Columbia. His early career was in business until he turned to research, writing, lecturing and teaching. He served with the Republican National Committee (1943–1945), and two committees of the U.S. Congress (1945–1947), the Joint Congressional Committee on the Investigation of the Pearl Harbor Attack and the House Education and Labor Committee. His principal assignments were with the Christian Freedom Foundation, The Freedom School, The Foundation for Economic Education and the University of Plano. He became seriously interested in the work of Professor Mises and attended Mises' New York University graduate seminar continuously from the fall of 1950 until the professor retired in the spring of 1969. *Mises Made Easier* is the product of Mr. Greaves' careful study of Mises' writings and his close association with the Professor.

This work is dedicated
to a better understanding and acceptance
of the great contributions to human knowledge

by

Ludwig von Mises.

As Mises says: "The first purpose of scientific terminology is to facilitate the analysis of the problems involved."
(*Human Action,* page 434)

It is, therefore, not so much a question as to whether the
definition is the popular one or not, but rather does it
lead the reader to a better understanding of the highly
complex ideas the author is trying to elucidate.

Foreword

Percy Greaves has asked me to write a few words as a foreword for his *Glossary* of Ludwig von Mises' HUMAN ACTION. I most willingly do so.

HUMAN ACTION is well known to me. I typed 980 pages of the manuscript. I shall never forget the concentration with which my husband worked, how carefully he chose every single word and fought with the editor about the slightest editorial change. He never gave in.

Professor von Mises always recognized the great importance of such a *Glossary*. It should make the reading of HUMAN ACTION easier and provide a fuller understanding of his ideas to a greater circle of readers and students. He appreciated the tremendous amount of work and the thoroughness with which Professor Greaves accomplished his task. I could not do better than repeat my husband's words when he commented on Percy Greaves' recent book, *Understanding The Dollar Crisis:* "I hope this book will be a great success."

MARGIT V. MISES
(Mrs. Ludwig von Mises)

June 24, 1974

Preface

Mises aptly named his economic treatise, HUMAN ACTION. It expounds in detail and with precision the human processes of social cooperation in a free or unhampered market society. It also sets forth with a similar precision the undesirable consequences that inevitably flow from every political interference with those voluntary social actions of men and women that are in keeping with the Golden Rule, i.e., actions which, barring force, fraud and human error, provide a psychic profit for all participants. It is truly the economics bible for all those who seek peace and prosperity not only for themselves but for all mankind. There is nothing like it in existence. However, its great contributions need to be made easier for average readers to digest, reflect upon and make part of their understanding and actions.

Henry Hazlitt, one of Mises' closest friends and a distinguished member of the elite few to whom Mises expressed his "thanks for very valuable and helpful suggestions," has written:

> "If any single book can turn the ideological tide that has been running in recent years so heavily toward statism, socialism and totalitarianism, HUMAN ACTION is that book. . . . It should become the leading text of everyone who believes in freedom, in individualism and in the ability of a free market economy not only to outdistance any government planned system in the production of goods and services for the masses, but to promote and safeguard, as no collectivist tyranny can ever do, those intellectual, cultural and moral values upon which all civilization ultimately rests."

The jacket for the first edition proclaimed HUMAN ACTION as "the counterweight of Marx's *Das Kapital,* of Lord Keynes' *Gen-*

ix

eral Theory, and of countless other books recommending social-
ization, planning, credit expansion and similar panaceas. Ludwig
von Mises is internationally known as the head of the 'Austrian
School' of economics, the teacher . . . of many other economists,
who largely through him have come to know economics as an
inquiry into human action, based on principles no less rigorous
than those of the physical sciences."

As the undersigned has written in his dedication of *Understanding the Dollar Crisis,* his recent attempt to put some of Mises'
fundamental contributions in an easily readable form, we all owe
much to Ludwig von Mises "whose contributions may yet save
our civilization."

It is thus extremely important that HUMAN ACTION not only be
read by present and future thought leaders but also that they read
it *with understanding.* As Professor Mises wrote and carefully
edited every page of HUMAN ACTION with scientific accuracy and
scholarly precision, he chose many terms and expressions with
which both lay readers and graduate students are generally unfamiliar. While his chosen words expressed exactly what he meant
to say, many readers, meeting them for the first time, fail to grasp
some of the fine, but important, points Mises was attempting to
make. Having an unabridged dictionary nearby is helpful, but not
always satisfactory, because few such dictionaries indicate the
precise sense in which Mises used many of these little understood
terms.

Many such words develop new and often differing meanings
with the passage of time. Take the terms "socialism" and "liberal,"
for example. The former term once included the voluntary cooperation of a relatively free society. More than a century ago, the
advocates of a politically-directed enforced cooperation, liking its
popular acceptance and pleasant connotations, called themselves
"socialists." In time they completely changed the accepted meaning of "socialism." Within the last century, the word "liberal" has
suffered the same 100 percent shift in popular meaning. Mises,
however, loyal to the word's original meaning, continued to use
the term "liberal" in its traditional sense, akin to liberty and not to
political compulsions. This *Glossary* provides his definition.

How many people read a book with a large dictionary handy?

Very few. When the author of this *Glossary* first read HUMAN ACTION, he traveled frequently and spent many a night reading in hotel rooms. Mass transit may provide soft music and even movies, but it seldom provides a Second Edition Unabridged *Webster Dictionary*. In hotels and motels, they are even scarcer. Few graduate students keep one in their study. For the average adult reader, the situation is often worse and who wants to visit a library as often as he finds a foreign phrase or an unfamiliar word in HUMAN ACTION.

The need to make the reading of HUMAN ACTION easier has existed for twenty-five years. A first primitive attempt was made as early as 1952 by the late Alvin Wingfield. With the aid of a large dictionary, he defined a number of the more difficult and less familiar terms for a North Carolina group that then met regularly to read and discuss HUMAN ACTION. His efforts were helpful but lacked a precise Misesian touch.

Early in 1964, after the First Edition of HUMAN ACTION had gone through six printings and a Revised Second Edition had appeared, the Foundation for Economic Education contemplated establishing a graduate course in economics. Dean Russell was in charge of the project. He contemplated using HUMAN ACTION as the text. With the blessings of Leonard Read, the Foundation's President, Dr. Russell approached the undersigned, as a Mises' disciple who had helped with the Second Edition revisions, and suggested he prepare a *Glossary of Human Action* for FEE's internal use and, perhaps, for wider distribution.

A start was made almost immediately. Later that year, a preliminary draft of definitions of words selected from the first 397 pages of the Second Edition was mimeographed and circulated privately for criticisms and suggestions. A number of helpful comments were received. Unquestionably, the most valuable assistance came from Professor Mises himself. He returned a copy marked up with his treasured handwritten suggestions which were quickly accepted as corrections.

Meanwhile, FEE's preliminary explorations of the possibility of a FEE graduate school resulted in a finding that it would be unable to grant degrees without being subject to the supervision and regulation of the New York State Board of Regents. Since such requirements were contrary to the freedom philosophy of Leonard Read, the graduate project was dropped and production of the completed *Glossary* delayed. However, the undersigned continued in his spare time the work he had started.

The author had first registered for the Mises graduate seminar at New York University in the fall of 1950 and was an active participant until its final session in May 1969. He also spent considerable time with Professor Mises, often driving him home from the seminar. This provided frequent opportunities to question the learned professor on many of the fine points of his contributions and the sense in which he used particular terms. Every difficult word, expression and foreign phrase in the Second Edition was underscored and defined. Countless dictionaries and reference books were consulted. Each definition was typed on a 4″ x 6″ card or as many such cards as were needed. They reflected the results of numerous readings of HUMAN ACTION, as well as all other Mises' writings available in the English language.

When the author considered the definitions satisfactorily completed, he left them with Professor Mises for his perusal. This was early in 1965, when Professor Mises was at the height of his great mental powers. Appointments were later made to meet with Professor Mises in his study on March 27, April 12, and May 4, 1965. We spent three hours together on each occasion for a total of nine hours. Professor Mises read the cards that interested him while making succinct and very pertinent comments. Careful notes were made of everything he said. In a few cases, he suggested specific sources for assistance. On occasion, he would remark that it would take a book or at least a chapter to do justice with a particular definition.

The time that Mises gave to the project was a good indication of the importance he attached to it. Each definition which had not met with his approval was carefully revised in line with his comments. It was he who suggested that the name of Friederich A. Hayek be added after his, as a then current leader of the Austrian School of Economics who, like the others, was Austrian born. Except for a few cards which were later discussed with him in detail, Professor Mises never saw the definitions again. Consequently, the author must assume full responsibility for those definitions which may not measure up to his high standards.

The *Glossary* was basically completed by the end of 1965. The author then started to add a section on the significance of each of the many persons and places mentioned in HUMAN ACTION. This proved to be a difficult and time consuming task, particularly as the contributions of many of those cited were in foreign languages and not readily available. The urgency of other matters resulted in the project remaining dormant for a number of years.

During the 1968-1969 academic year, this professor used HUMAN ACTION as a text for fourth year economics students. The then available *Glossary* was typed and duplicated for student use. Although the copies contained many typographical errors, they proved to be very helpful in the reading and classroom discussions of HUMAN ACTION. On special request other duplications were later made for strictly private use.

Over the years many people have urged that the *Glossary* be made available in book form. With the passing of Professor Mises on October 10, 1973, it was decided to get the *Glossary* into print in 1974, the twenty-fifth anniversary of the First Edition of HUMAN ACTION. The idea of including an addendum on persons and places was dropped. Among those most insistent that the *Glossary* be more generally available has been Señor Joaquin Reig Albiol, the translator into Spanish of the First and Third Editions of HUMAN ACTION. He has also kindly offered financial assistance and indicated a strong desire to make the *Glossary* available in Spanish. The author's wife, Bettina Bien Greaves, a member of the Senior Staff of the Foundation for Economic Education, has also urged that the *Glossary* be completed in final form and published. She offered to retype the *Glossary* cards in manuscript form and assist with the many details of checking and proof reading.

With this encouragement, the definitions were reread in late 1973. Page references to HUMAN ACTION were changed from those of the Second Edition to those of the Third Edition. Finishing touches were added to the few definitions that needed to be brought up to date. The saddest addition was filling in the years for our late great teacher (1881-1973). References to Mises have been left in the present tense as his thoughts will always be with us.

* * * * * *

This *Glossary* should not only make it easier for readers to grasp the full significance of Mises' contributions in his great treatise, but it is also an economics text in its own right. It presents many of Mises' concepts in both a readable and convenient form. Mises often, too often, assumed that those who read or heard him could understand his message. He frequently wrote and spoke for students of the graduate level, with the belief that those interested had already familiarized themselves with his earlier writings. Unfortunately, this assumption was often contrary to fact. Long after this author had read HUMAN ACTION many times, he needed more contact with Professor Mises before he could ferret out his finer meanings. Mises saw these fine points so clearly that he found it difficult to realize that others, without his extraordinary acumen and encyclopedic knowledge, could not grasp them at a first reading.

This *Glossary* provides the reader with the answers in succinct form to many of the popular economic fallacies of our times. It also provides the reader with a ready reference to the pages in Mises' English writings in which he discusses in some detail the subject of the definition. It is thus hoped that it will make it easier for thought leaders to grasp the full significance of Mises' great contributions, contributions which "may yet save our civilization." If this *Glossary* should encourage a modicum of scholars to pursue a serious study of the free market society and all the writings of Mises, this author will feel he has made a small down payment on the huge debt he personally owes his late great teacher.

* * * * * *

On page 488 of the Third Edition of HUMAN ACTION, Mises has a section entitled "Observations on the Evolution of the Time Preference Theory." A footnote thereto refers the reader to his *Nationalökonomie* (1940) "for a detailed critical analysis of this part of Böhm-Bawerk's reasoning." This reference has not been available in English and the book is not likely to be translated, because its contents, for the most part, have already appeared in

xiv

HUMAN ACTION. Consequently, this author long ago asked Mrs. Greaves to translate this important passage needed for a complete reading and understanding of Mises' position on interest. The passage has recently been reworked and this author has edited it into a form he believes Mises would have approved. It is included with this *Glossary* as a useful addendum for the serious Mises student.

Two years before Mises died, he sanctioned the translation of three of his short German works by Bettina Bien Greaves. These works all deal with the monetary problem which remains the greatest threat to our civilization. Their availability will be another great aid to those who seek to understand this very complicated problem. They are:

> *The Stabilization Problem from the Viewpoint of Monetary Theory (Die geldtheoretische Seite des Stabilisierungsproblems)*, January 1923;
> *Monetary Stabilization and Cyclical Policy (Geldwertstabilisierung und Konjunkturpolitik)*, 1928; and
> *The Causes of the Economic Crisis: An Address (Die Ursachen der Wirtschaftskrise)*, February 28, 1931.

In his letter of September 24, 1971, to Mrs. Greaves, he kindly added:

> "It is my further request that your translations be carefully reviewed and edited by your husband, Percy L. Greaves, Jr., to assure that they present, as far as possible, a faithful English language interpretation of my ideas originally expressed in German."

The translations having been completed, the pleasant chore of editing these works will now become the order of the day.

Before closing this Preface, the author wishes to thank Dean Russell, Leonard Read and the Foundation for Economic Education for their part and help in getting this project underway. Thanks are also due Mrs. Bette Fletcher and Mrs. Virginia Clifford, who typed with great care a large number of the original cards. The author is also indebted to Mr. and Mrs. Roger Sharlow who typed the 1968-1969 version of the *Glossary* and to Mr. Bart Carley who taped the classroom discussions of the HUMAN ACTION course in which the *Glossary* was used. The author must also thank his beloved wife for her encouragement, which at times might more precisely be called "goading," and for her assistance with the typing, proofing and myriads of other necessary details. She has contributed much of her time and knowledge to help make an understanding of Mises easier for the reader of this *Glossary*.

In closing, the author wishes to stress again the sentiment with which he ended his remarks at the Commitment of the late Ludwig von Mises on October 13, 1973. May this *Glossary* help further the influence of his name and works through the ages.

PERCY L. GREAVES, JR.

June 9, 1974

P.S. The author wants to express his gratitude to Mrs. Ludwig von Mises for her graciousness in writing the Foreword. He must also acknowledge with thanks that it is due to the generosity of some Spanish friends of Professor Mises and this author that this *Glossary* appears in such a fine form.

P.L.G., Jr.

P.P.S. Since the first edition of this book appeared in 1974, the three German monographs mentioned on page xv have been published, *On the Manipulation of Money and Credit* (Free Market Books, 1978). Mises' discussions there of "Balance of payments," "Free banking," "Index numbers," "Inflation," and the "Trade cycle" are especially helpful.

In my husband's working copy of this book, I found notes of several changes he would have made in a new edition:

"Civil War" (p. 20) Revised in this edition to correct an erroneous statement about the populations of the North and the South.

"Contradictio in adjecto" (p. 25) He would have added the synonym, "oxymoron."

"Economics" (p. 37) He would have added another reference, "HA. 878–879."

The prominent Mexican lawyer, Gustavo R. Velasco, suggested that "Economic calculation" be defined. As I am sure my husband would have followed Lic. Velasco's suggestion, a definition of that phenomenon has been added, based like the other definitions in this book on Mises' teachings. See Appendix B, p. 158.

For a word on new editions of Mises' pertinent works, see page xviii. Otherwise, no changes have been made in this second edition.

B.B.G.

June 1990

References

For those desiring further amplification of the subjects defined, frequent references are made to the pertinent pages in the writings of Mises, as well as in this author's recent book. The abbreviations for Mises' books, presently available in English, follow:

AC—*The Anti-Capitalistic Mentality* (Van Nostrand, 1956; Libertarian Press, 1972)

AS —*The Historical Setting of the Austrian School of Economics* (Arlington House, 1969)

B —*Bureaucracy* (Yale, 1944; Arlington House, 1969)

EP —*Epistemological Problems of Economics* (Van Nostrand, 1960)

FC —*The Free and Prosperous Commonwealth* (Van Nostrand, 1962)

HA—*Human Action,* 3rd ed. (Regnery, 1966)

M —*The Theory of Money and Credit* (Yale, 1953; Foundation for Economic Education, 1971)

OG—*Omnipotent Government* (Yale, 1944; Arlington House, 1969)

PF —*Planning for Freedom,* 2nd ed. (Libertarian Press, 1962)

S —*Socialism* (Yale, 1951; Jonathan Cape, 1969)

TH—*Theory and History* (Yale, 1957; Arlington House, 1969)

UF—*The Ultimate Foundation of Economic Science* (Van Nostrand, 1962)

The abbreviation used for the author's book is:

PLG—*Understanding the Dollar Crisis* (Western Islands, 1973)

KEY TO OTHER ABBREVIATIONS

adj.—adjective.

Ch.—Chapter.

e.g.—exempli gratia (Latin),
    for example.

et al—et alii (Latin), and others.

i.e.—id est (Latin), that is.

n.—noun.

p. or pp.—page or pages.

pl.—plural.

q.v.—quod vide (Latin),
    which see.

v.—verb.

NOTE: Titles and paging of new editions of Mises' works may vary. See, for instance, *The Free and Prosperous Commonwealth*, abbreviated here as "FC," reissued under its original title, *Liberalism* (Sheed, Andrews & McMeel, 1978; Foundation for Economic Education and Cobden Press, 1985). *The Theory of Money and Credit* and *Socialism*, with type completely reset and pages renumbered, have been published in new editions by Liberty Fund (1980 and 1981 respectively).

A

Abortive. Ineffective, implying failure before action has begun or been completed.

Absolutization. The act, state or condition of unlimited and unconditional power or sovereignty.

Acta Borussica, (Latin). The title given to the tomes containing a collection of official documents concerning the history of the Electorate of Brandenberg and the Kingdom of Prussia. Published by the Prussian Archives, these volumes were prepared under the supervision of Gustav von Schmoller (1838-1917), a leader of the Historical School (q.v.). NOTE: *Borussica* was the original name for the area that became Prussia.

Action directe, (French). Literally, direct action. The syndicalist Georges Sorel (1847-1922), rejecting the "peaceful" tactics of the socialist parties and labor unions, advocated a radical change in "working class" policies in the form of *action directe,* i.e., violent action aiming at the destruction of what was called the "bourgeois" system of economic management. See "Syndicalism."
AC. 109-110; S. 545.

Ad hoc, (Latin). For a particular purpose or occasion, usually specified.

Ad libitum, (Latin). Freely; at one's pleasure; as one wishes.

Adventitious. Extrinsic; not essentially inherent; arising from an external source not the essence of the subject; not naturally, normally or historically associated with the subject or event.

Age of Enlightenment. Pretty much the same period and development for which the "Age of Reason" is also used. It stretched roughly from John Locke (1632-1704) and Isaac Newton (1642-1727) to Immanuel Kant (1724-1804). During this period there was a great advance in all branches of human knowledge.

Age of Reason.   The eighteenth century, particularly in England and France, when reason rather than emotion, intuition or superstition was presumed to have prevailed.

Agnosticism.   The doctrine that refuses to accept the evidence of revelation and holds that it is impossible to prove or disprove the existence of God. Hence, any doctrine which holds the impossibility of any true knowledge, such as the doctrine that all knowledge is relative.

Alter ego, (Latin).   Literally, "other I," another self. A fellow man considered as one who thinks and acts "as I, the Ego, do."

American Revolution (1776-1783).   See "Revolution, American."

Anarchism.   The idea that peaceful social cooperation can continue to exist without the institution of government, the social apparatus of coercion and compulsion.
   FC. 36-37; HA. 149; OG. 48; UF. 98-99

Anarchy.   Lawlessness; condition of no government or ruling power.
   S. 548.

Anarchy of production.   A Marxian phrase for production in a nonsocialist society as, for example, in a market economy.
   PF. 104.

Anchorite.   One who renounces the world and lives both a solitary and secluded life of prayer, penitence and meditation.

Ancien régime, (French).   The old regime; the former social and political order or system. The term usually refers to the period preceding the French Revolution of 1789.

Ancillary.   Auxiliary; assisting in a subordinate or subservient manner.

Animism, n. ani.nistic, adj.   The theory that all beings and objects have a soul. Animism ascribes to all things of the universe the faculty of action, similar to that of man.

UF. 36.

Annona, (Latin). A policy of the Roman Empire (27 B.C.- 476 A.D.), whereby the government distributed free of charge the most important foods—grain, wine and oil—to the poor city people. This policy encouraged people to flock to the cities where living was cheap and eventually necessitated heavy imports of grain.

Anthropocentrism. The belief that man is the center of all that is important and that the world exists solely for the benefit or improvement of mankind.

Anthropomorphism. The idea that ascribes to God, or a god, the characteristics of a human being.

Antichrematistic. The opposite of chrematistic (q.v.).

Antinomy. Contradiction of two principles deduced from premises considered to be equally valid.

Antithesis, n. **antithetic,** adj. Diametrically opposite. A word, idea, person, doctrine, proposition or thing that negates, is irreconcilable with, or represents the extreme opposite of another.

Apodictic. Logically necessary, or the logical necessity of which can be demonstrated.

Apostasy. Abandonment or repudiation of a previously held faith, principle or party loyalty.

A posteriori, (Latin). Literally, following after. Known from experience. Applied to inductive reasoning, beginning with observed facts and inferring general conclusions from these. Opposed to *a priori* (q.v.). See also "Induction."

UF. 18.

Appellation. A name or term by which a person, group, theory or thing is known, with some implication that it is a popular or descriptive substitute for the real one.

Apperception. In epistemology, the human mind's awareness or

3

understanding of its own contents. In psychology, the process whereby the human mind integrates new experiences with past experiences to form a new composite unity of understanding.

Appraisal, appraisement. An impersonal judgment, often by a disinterested expert, of the price something would bring if sold in the market place.
HA. 332.

Après nous le déluge, (French). "After us the deluge." A statement Madame de Pompadour (1721-1764) is reputed to have made on November 5, 1757, to King Louis XV (1710-1774) of France, after the army of Frederick the Great (1712-1786) of Prussia had routed the much larger combined forces of the French and her allies at Rossbach (near Leipzig, Germany). See "Seven Years War."

A priori, (Latin). Literally, from the former or preceding. Self-evident knowledge known by reason alone without any appeal to experience or sensory perceptions. Nonempirical. Opposed to *a posteriori* (q.v.).
An *a priori* statement is one which the human mind can neither question nor contradict and which cannot be further analyzed, diagnosed, broken down or traced back to a logically prior cause. It is thus the original datum or premise which forms the starting point for deductive reasoning.
HA. 34; UF. 17-21, 54.

Apriorism. The doctrine that there is knowledge that is logically prior to experience (or sensory perceptions).

Arbitrage. The process of buying commodities, securities or foreign exchange for immediate or future delivery in one market and simultaneously, or almost simultaneously, selling them in another market in order to profit from the price differences in the two markets. This process almost immediately eliminates all price differences in different markets except for those due to transportation costs and political interventions (taxes, tariffs, etc.).

A rebours, (French). The wrong way; backwards; against the grain.

Argumentum a contrario, (Latin). Argument or proof by contrast or the direct opposite.

Artel, (Russian). Literally, a gang. Actually, a group of workmen joined together for the cooperative performance of a work project and the mutual sharing of the income received. The custom arose when groups of workers left rural areas for the towns and cities where they worked, ate and lived together as a family sharing income and expenses. They elected a leader who supervised all activities and dealt with employers or contractors. Some *artels* were formed for temporary jobs like building a house, bridge or road. Others were more like fraternal guilds or craft unions with as many as 200 members pooling their wages. Before the Communist Revolution of 1918, they operated not only in crafts, construction and industry but also in fishing, forestry, banking and even in prisons and stock exchanges. Under the Soviet regime, *artels* are largely confined to communal farms where the workers live together.

Artifact. A natural object modified by human art, applied largely to primitive tools, weapons and works of art. An object which human labor has improved or made useful as distinguished from one as originally found in nature.

Asceticism. The theory that the only means open to man for attaining complete quietude, contentment and happiness is to renounce all earthly concerns and worldly things in preparation for eternal bliss. Only an ascetic may reproach liberalism for advancing the outward material welfare of men.
    FC. 4-5; HA. 178-179.

Asymptotic. Approaching indefinitely near, yet never meeting.

ἀταραξία, (*Ataraxia,* Greek). Complete peace of mind.
    HA. 15.

Atavistic. Pertaining to or marked by atavism, the recurrence in a descendant of abnormal characteristics that can be traced back to a remote ancestor. More popularly, "throwback."

Atypical. Deviating markedly from the rule or standard; not typical or regular; above or below average.

Aurea aetas, (Latin).   Golden Age.

Aureole.   A halo or celestial crown meant to indicate sanctity or holiness; a spiritual reward for those who have maintained their integrity and triumphed over worldly temptations.

Austrian School (of Economics).   A group of economists who developed the modern subjective theory of value and applied it to the various problems of economics. Its founders and early leaders—Carl Menger (1840-1921), Friedrich von Wieser (1851-1926), and Eugen von Böhm-Bawerk (1851-1914), as well as Ludwig (von) Mises (1881-1973) and Friedrich A. Hayek (1899-   )— were all Austrian born. See Mises' *The Historical Setting of the Austrian School of Economics* (1969).
EP. 165.

Autarky, (popularly misspelled "autarchy").   The state or condition of a person, nation or geographic area of being economically or intellectually self-sufficient and thus not dependent on another for trade, knowledge or survival.
OG. 72-78, 250, 284-286.

Autistic.   Involving only one person or individual; excluding all but the one person.

Autochthonous.   Native; indigenous; aboriginal; springing from the soil or land; related to the original primitive inhabitants.

Automatism.   The theory that living organisms are governed solely by the laws of physics and mechanics. An extreme form of behaviorism that denies conscious control of actions.

Autonomy, n. **autonomous,** adj.   Independence; the right or power to be self-governing; the state or quality of being free from outside control.

B

Babbittry. A derogatory term for the ethics and practices of small independent businessmen operating under the relatively free market conditions existing in the United States before the massive governmental interventions of the 1920's and 1930's. The term comes from the novel *Babbitt* (1922) in which the author, Sinclair Lewis (1885-1951), derides the behavior and character of George Follansbee Babbitt, a fictional middle class realtor.

Balance of payments. The separate and reciprocal summation of the monetary figures for (1) the goods, including money, and services given, and (2) the goods, including money, and services received by an individual or a group of individuals, as frequently those living within national or other geographical boundaries during any particular period of time. Since the monetary figures for both the items received (debit side) and the items given (credit side) are always equal, the two summations (of payments) are likewise always equal, i.e., in balance.

It is customary to list and subtotal separately the monetary and nonmonetary items. If the monetary receipts exceed the monetary outflow, the balance of payments is said to be *favorable*. If the monetary outflow exceeds the monetary receipts, the balance of payments is said to be *unfavorable*. This is a carry-over from the days of mercantilism (q.v.) when the precious metals were considered more valuable than any other goods or services. This viewpoint, still widely accepted, ignores the fact that at the time of every transaction, each party prefers and considers of greater value the item he receives, whether it is money, other goods or services. Thus, no one ever pays out money unless he prefers what he receives in return.

During periods when a nation is substituting fiduciary media (q.v.) for a part of its monetary stock (gold), Gresham's law (q.v.) goes into operation and the nation experiences a net outflow of its monetary stock (gold), i.e., an unfavorable balance of payments.
HA. 450-458; M. 249; OG. 215, 218-219.

Banking School. This group was opposed by the Currency School (q.v.) in the nineteenth century controversy over the laws which should govern the Bank of England and form the basis of the British monetary system. Drawing on the writings of Adam Smith (1723-1790), the Banking School espoused what has become known as the "Banking Principle" or "Principle of Fullarton." This principle holds that as long as a bank maintains the convertibility of its banknotes into specie (gold), for which it should keep "adequate" reserves, it is impossible for it to overissue its banknotes against sound commercial paper with fixed short term (90 days or less) maturities.

The Banking School reasoned that under these conditions, the issuance of such banknotes was helpful to business activity, did not raise prices, and the quantity issuable would be independently determined and limited by the needs of trade (business) rather than the desires of the issuing bank. They claimed that noteholders would promptly present for redemption all banknotes issued in excess of the needs of trade (business) under the so-called "law of reflux." Some held that the "banking principle" was valid even if convertibility was not maintained.

The Banking School adherents failed to realize that the banks were free to increase the demand for their fiduciary banknotes by reducing the interest rate charged on bank loans. The British Bank (Peel's) Act of 1844 prohibited the issuance of further banknotes by the Bank of England against anything except 100% gold reserves. However, the Act did permit the expansion of demand deposits subject to transfer or withdrawal by check against short term commercial paper of the type approved by the "banking principle." This paved the way for currently popular banking theories based on fractional reserves, "elastic currency," circulation credit and credit expansion (q.v.). For the consequences, see "Monetary theory of the trade cycle."

8

Because no short definition can be fully satisfactory, the reader is urged to read the references.

HA. 439-441, 444, 571; M. 305-312, 343-345, 368-370; also PLG. 175-193. See also J. Laurence Laughlin's *The Principles of Money* (N.Y.: Chas. Scribner's Sons, 1903/1926), pp. 238-281; and Lloyd W. Mints' *A History of Banking Theory, in Great Britain and the United States* (Univ. of Chicago Press, 1945), pp. 74-124.

Banknotes. Money-substitutes issued by banks in the form of non-interest bearing promissory notes, payable to bearer on demand, which circulate freely as a substitute for the sum of money stated on their face. Banknotes differ from fiat money in that fractional reserves (less than 100%) are kept by the issuing bank or its agents for their redemption. Banknotes are money-substitutes and "money in the broader sense." Only the reserves held for their redemption are "money in the narrower sense." The amount of banknotes issued in excess of the reserves maintained for their redemption is fiduciary media (q.v.).

HA. 432-448, 460, 571; M. 52-59, 271-275, 278-280, 319-321, 439, 482-483.

Bank of England. The central bank of the United Kingdom. It was granted its original charter in 1694 in return for a £1,200,000 loan at 8% interest to the British government. The charter permitted it to issue £1,200,000 of Bank of England notes redeemable on demand in gold, supposedly obtainable from funds deposited with the Bank. It has always acted as the government's banker. During the first half of the nineteenth century, the Bank's policies were discussed and investigated in detail by British economists. (See "Banking School" and "Currency School.") The Peel Act of 1844 (q.v.) set up separate departments for the Bank's banking and note issue functions.

Up until World War I, it was the unquestioned symbol of financial integrity and the stability of the gold standard. Since 1925, it has enjoyed a monopoly in the issue of banknotes. Originally a private institution, it was nationalized in 1946. Its banknotes have full legal tender power. The Bank serves as fiscal agent for the British government and maintains reserves for countries in the

"Sterling Bloc" (q.v.). It performs all functions of a central bank (q.v.), and it is responsible for controlling the quantity of British money. For a short history of the British pound, see "Pound sterling."

Barbarian. Originally from the Greek for foreigners, meaning those who spoke an unintelligible language and had outlandish manners. It has come to mean a rude, crude, untutored, uncultured, cruel, almost savage person who is ignorant of civilized customs and human dignity.

OG. 123.

Bear. A financial term for a person who, anticipating lower prices, sells for future delivery a commodity, currency or security which he does not own with the expectation he will be able to buy it at a lower price before he is required to make delivery. A bear is said to sell short. The operations or transactions of bears have the effect on market prices of an increased supply and thus tend to reduce prices.

Begriffsjurisprudenz, (German). Literally, ideal jurisprudence. A school of German jurists which believed that ideal laws are based on a logical analysis of legal concepts.

Behaviorism. A sociological school which asserts that human minds are not capable of making rational choices. It studies human action according to the methods of animal and infant psychology. It seeks to investigate reflexes and instincts, automatisms and unconscious reactions, without reference to consciousness and aiming at end. Behaviorists consider all human actions to be implicit reactions to prior conditioning. They seek to improve mankind by subjecting people to an "ideal" conditioning from birth. In choosing such an "ideal" conditioning, the behaviorists would be acting in violation of their basic concept that all human actions are determined by some automatic mechanism.

TH. 245-246.

Bellicosity. Desire or disposition to stir up a fight or be warlike; inclination to be aggressive.

Bernoulli's doctrine *de mensura sortis*. Daniel Bernoulli (1700-

1782), an eminent mathematician and physical scientist, realized that equal or proportional changes in man's wealth or "physical fortune" did not produce equal or proportional changes in utility or satisfaction, which he called "moral fortune," and that such changes in "moral fortune" were related to his previous wealth or fortune as well as the physical changes in it. Accordingly, he resorted to logarithms to develop a mathematical formula or doctrine for computing the expectation of changes in "moral fortunes" that would result from any given physical changes in any person's previously held fortune. The suppositions of this doctrine were dependent upon the selection of arbitrary constants for human valuations. However, such valuations are not only unmeasurable but also variable from man to man and for the same man at different times. In distinguishing between "physical" and "moral" fortunes, Bernoulli's contribution made it clear that simple arithmetic (addition and subtraction) is not applicable to problems involving human valuations of different physical quantities.

Bill of exchange.   A negotiable document drawn up and signed by one party (usually, but not necessarily, a seller) on a second party (usually a buyer) providing that the second party unconditionally promises to pay to the order of bearer or a third party, but which may be the drawer or first party, a specified sum on sight (upon acceptance by the second party) or upon a specified or determinable date. The bill becomes valid only upon the signed acceptance by the second party. A bill payable at a future date is a credit instrument discountable at banks in advance of maturity, depending upon the credit of the parties signing the bill. At certain times and places in history, bills of exchange have been used as media of exchange. See "Medium of exchange."
   M. 52-53.

Bimetallism.   A monetary system which attempts to maintain a fixed exchange ratio between the metals gold and silver. For the failure of such attempts, see HA. 471-476, 781-783; M. 74-76; also PLG. 149-154.

Biological competition.   The antagonistic rivalry in which living beings are engaged in a life and death struggle for a part of the existing means of survival which are insufficient for the minimum

11

needs of all. This situation is inherent in nature and among wild animals incapable of social cooperation. It can exist among men (1) in those rare instances where the means of survival are insufficient for total survival for groups which are lost or otherwise isolated from civilization, or (2) where men fail to realize that the voluntary social cooperation of an unhampered market economy can increase the supply of scarce goods beyond the quantity needed for the general survival of a growing but intelligently limited population.

HA. 273-274, 667-672; TH. 38-40; UF. 88.

Bohemian. A devotee of art, music, literature or other intellectual pursuits who attempts to show his disdain for social conventions by adopting an odd or bizarre mode of life or dress.

AC. 108.

Bolshevik, (Russian). Literally, "a member of the majority." Actually, a Russian revolutionary communist. The term acquired this meaning in 1903 when the Russian Social Democratic Party split into the "Bolshevik" and "Menshevik" (q.v.) factions. In the Russian Revolution of November 1917, the Bolsheviks, under the leadership of Nikolai Lenin (1870-1924), overturned the Provisional Government established earlier that year and founded the Union of Soviet Socialist Republics.

AC. 109; OG. 51, 176-179; PF. 77-78; S. 547-549, 553, 557, 561, 563, 567, 570-571.

Bona fide, (Latin). In good faith; real; true; authentic; genuine.

Bourgeois, n. or adj., **bourgeoisie,** n. (French). The merchants, professional persons (doctors, lawyers, professors), employers and white collar workers, as distinguished from: (1) The clergy; (2) The nobility and the landed gentry; and (3) The manual workers and peasants called the proletariat. See "Proletarian."

Bourse, (French). A continental European stock exchange. As a rule such stock exchanges also trade in foreign exchange. The term also applies to commodity exchanges.

Bretton Woods Conference (and Agreement). The United Nations Monetary and Financial Conference called by President

Franklin D. Roosevelt (1882-1945). Representatives of 44 countries met at Bretton Woods, New Hampshire, July 1-22, 1944. The Conference approved agreements for the "International Monetary Fund" (q.v.) and the "International Bank for Reconstruction and Development" which was to provide financial assistance for "war-torn" and "underdeveloped regions." The idea for an international stabilization fund and an international bank originated with the U.S. government in the fall of 1941. After several years of technical preparation and preliminary international discussions, tentative proposals were readied for the Conference. The American proposal was prepared under the direction of Harry Dexter White (1892-1948) who died mysteriously shortly after being exposed as a Communist. The British draft was largely the work of Lord Keynes (1883-1946). See "Keynesians."

British Labor Party. See "Labor Party (British)."

Bucolic. Pastoral; relating to a shepherd's life or rural affairs.

Buddhism, Buddhist monks. An ancient religion in most Asian countries except for Siberia and the Arab lands. It was started by Gautama Buddha (563?-?483 B.C.) whose teachings have been variously interpreted and emphasized by the many different subdivisions or sects. Members are in general asked to live peaceful, highly moral lives of self-denial while treating even their enemies and animals with respect. A Buddhist believes that when his body dies, his soul is reborn in another body and retains the sorrows of previous sins. Good Buddhists are generous almsgivers.

Buddhist monks live in poverty on the gifts received from others. They must obey strict rules requiring great patience, pacifism and abstinence. They are taught that life is full of pain and sorrow due to man's desires, lusts, cravings and passions. They seek the highest possible bliss, or Nirvana, in the complete elimination from their lives of these inherent characteristics of human nature.

Bullion. Monetary metals as merchandise in any form but that of standard coins. Gold and silver bullion are usually in the form of bars or ingots, but they may also be in the form of refined ores or nonstandard coins, such as worn or foreign coins that are valued solely for their weight and fineness.

Bull market. Period of rising prices on the stock exchange and/ or commodity markets. Period of optimism in the financial markets with a general expectation of still higher prices in the future. A bull market is usually accompanied by an upsurge in buying on margin, i.e., buyers borrowing a part of the funds with which they pay for their purchases.

Bureaucrat. An employee or official whose actions and duties are guided and determined by rules, regulations and budgetary specifications established by law or other higher authority. The employment of bureaucrats and bureaucratic management is the only appropriate method for handling governmental affairs, for which market processes, economic calculation and the profit motive are unable to provide sufficient guidelines.

    B. particularly 57-63; HA. 308-311; PF. 113

Burgher. A freeman or inhabitant who enjoys all the privileges of a citizen of a town or borough.

Business cycle. See "Trade cycle."

C

Caesarism. Political dictatorship; absolute government under one-man rule; one-man imperialism. The term comes from Gaius Julius Caesar (100 B.C.-44 B.C.), a general who expanded the Roman Empire and became its dictator, even though refusing a crown.

Capital. The fundamental concept of economic calculation which expresses in monetary terms the net wealth (assets minus liabilities) of the complex of all kinds of capital goods and marketable assets (savings) belonging to a definite person or other unit participating in a market economy. It is only by use of such an accounting concept that (1) profits (increases in capital account) and losses (decreases in capital account) of contemplated market actions can be estimated or prognosticated, and (2) profits and losses of completed actions can be calculated. Thus the mental tool of capital is essential both as a compass for guiding future market actions and as a means for evaluating the success or non-success of completed market actions.

HA. 260-264, 491; PF. 110-125.

Capital accumulation. The act, process or result of creating or increasing the supply of capital goods (q.v.). Capital can only be accumulated by producing more wealth than is consumed, i.e., saving.

AC. 38-43, 82-89; HA. 490-493, 774-775; OG. 101-102; PF. 181.

Capital consumption (or decumulation). The act or process of consuming or reducing the supply of capital goods (q.v.).

HA. 490-493; PF. 181.

Capital flight. The popular idea that invested wealth leaves one country for another. While gold and other commodities always move to those markets placing the highest value on them, neither invested wealth (capital goods) nor a nation's irredeemable paper money leaves a country. Only their values "flee," usually because investors (capitalists), as a result of new information or fears, have readjusted downward their appraisal of the future values of such

15

investments (securities or monetary units). Investors profit from such a situation only when they correctly anticipate changes in the future market values before they actually occur. Capital flight is actually a loss in confidence that results in a drop in values.
HA. 517-520.

Capital goods. Produced factors of production, such as tools, buildings, transportation facilities, partially finished goods, and both cash and consumers goods which make it possible for the owner to engage in more time-consuming and more productive processes of wealth production than would be possible if he did not possess such forms of saving. In short, stored up labor, natural resources and time in the form of economic goods whose possession reduces the time necessary to attain some goal of human endeavor.
AC. 84-89; HA. 259-261, 490-493; PF. 111, 120.

Capitalism. An economic concept of civilization that is based on the private ownership (and control) of the means of production. Such an institutional situation permits and inevitably encourages the division of labor, economic calculation, capital accumulation, technological improvement and the voluntary social cooperation of a market economy in which mass production is designed for the consumption of the sovereign masses. Capitalism is the antithesis of statism, socialism and communism which are based on government ownership (or control) of the means of production.
AC. 1-33, 48-112; B. 10, 18, 20-39, 67, 93, 105, 118-119; OG. 49-50, 284.

Capital levy. A tax or assessment imposed on privately held property, usually nonrecurring.

Carmen. A grand opera composed by Georges Bizet (1838-1875), with libretto by Meilhac (1831-1897) and Ludovic Halévy (1834-1908), and based on a romantic novel of the same name by Prosper Merimée (1803-1870).

Cartel. An association of business firms in any one industry, which is formed for the purpose of limiting competition in order to substitute monopoly prices (q.v.) for competitive prices. Without government assistance, cartels could exist only in those few cases where nature has limited the sources of a raw commodity to easily controlled narrow geographic areas, but such instances are rare (possibly diamonds and mercury) and thus could play only a minor role in world trade and production. Cartels were used primarily in pre-World War II Germany to protect domestic industries, heavily burdened with welfare state taxes (social security, etc.) from competition with foreign firms not so burdened. The cartel device permits industries to sell abroad at competitive prices while charging monopoly prices in the domestic market that are sufficiently high to cover the welfare state expenses on total sales and production, thus placing the entire burden on domestic consumers. The agricultural programs of the American government are a substitute for a cartel.

HA. 365-368; OG. 70-77.

Car tel est notre bon plaisir, (French).   For such is our good pleasure. A phrase frequently used by monarchs when signing a law.

Catallactic competition.   The peaceful competition of the market economy wherein each participant seeks his own satisfaction in striving to excel in some contribution that will best satisfy the needs or desires of his fellow participants in a market society. Catallactic competition tends to produce the greatest possible satisfaction of consumers by assigning each individual in a voluntary society that function in which he can render to all his fellow men the most valuable of the services he is able to perform.

HA. 117, 274-279; UF. 88.

Catallactics, n. **catallactic,** adj.   The theory of the market economy, i.e., of exchange ratios and prices. It analyzes all actions based on monetary calculation and traces the formation of prices back to the point where acting man makes his choices. It explains market prices as they are and not as they should be. The laws of catallactics are not value judgments, but are exact, objective and of universal validity.

EP. 88-89, 149, 208; HA. 234, 327-328, 646, 650, 652.

Catallactic unemployment.   See "Unemployment, catallactic."

Caucasian.   A large and rather indefinite division of mankind which in the eighteenth century was comprised of the chief races of Europe, North Africa and Southwest Asia. All mankind was divided into five species by Johann F. Blumenbach (1752-1840) in

17

1781. The other four were Mongolian, Ethiopian, American and Malay.

Central bank. An ideal type (q.v.) rather than a scientific term since no two central banks are precisely alike.

Almost all modern countries have a central bank which is a large bank operating either as a direct governmental institution or as a private institution whose management is strictly controlled by the government. Most central banks were established by law as the result of a national financial emergency, such as the collapse of a prior credit expansion (U.S. Federal Reserve Banks), or the desire of the government for more funds than it cares or dares to raise through taxes or private loans (Bank of England). Central banks usually attempt to control interest rates, reserve requirements and note issues of the nation's banks and act as the bank of last resort when other banks are pressed for funds while holding investments which the central bank will discount on demand. By such technical procedures, the central bank attempts to control the quantity of "money in the broader sense" (q.v.) and thus indirectly influence prices, production and employment. Central bank policies are usually determined by a desire to (1) prevent financial panics, recessions or depressions, usually by the expansion of circulation credit (q.v.), and (2) provide the government with funds to cover any deficits not fully covered by funds from private sources.

M. 422.

"Ce que j'appelle mon present, c'est mon attitude vis-a-vis de l'avenir immediat, c'est mon action imminente," (French). "What I call my present is my mental attitude towards the immediate future, my imminent action."

Ceteris paribus, (Latin). Other things (factors or elements) being equal or remaining unchanged. *Ceteris paribus* is an element of every scientific doctrine and no economic law can dispense with it.

M. 129.

Charisma, (Greek). A special divine gift which endows the recipient with a supernatural ability to know and proclaim the will of God. In short, a pipeline from God which mere mortals may not challenge.

Chauvinism. Absurdly exaggerated patriotism or militarism; originally a term of ridicule applied to idolatry of Napoleon I (1769-1821), it came from the name of Nicolas Chauvin, a much wounded and decorated veteran who worshipped with blind enthusiasm the military glories and expansionist policies of his defeated hero.

Chauvinism applies to talk and disposition. It thus differs from nationalism which applies to a policy of action. For distinction, see *Omnipotent Government,* pp. 122-125.

OG. 1, 122-125.

Checkbook money. See "Deposit currency."

Chiliastic. Pertaining to the doctrine that when men are perfected the Messiah will appear on the Earth to rule over a happy and glorious kingdom for 1,000 years (the Millennium).

S. 281-288.

Chimera. Originally a fabled and frightening monster whose features resembled the corresponding parts of many different animals. Hence, an absurd or fantastic creature of the imagination; a frightful fancy; a visionary or impracticable idea.

Chimerical. Wildly or fantastically unreal or visionary.

Chrematistic. Related to wealth as far as it can be calculated in terms of money.

Christian socialism. A brand of socialism that seeks to base the socialist system upon loyalty to the Christian church as opposed to antireligious, anti-Christian, atheistic brands of socialism. It emerged in the nineteenth century and is based primarily on disapproval of the desire for profits or personal gain. Its advocates generally ignore the problem of production, oppose bigness and radical innovations in business and seek what they consider a "more just" allocation of existing wealth. They yearn for "just" prices and wages, usually those of some point in the past for which the only hope of maintenance lies in a completely controlled economy.

S. 252-258, 423-429.

Circulation credit. Credit extended by banks in the form of banknotes or demand deposits especially created for this purpose; as opposed to credit granted by the loan of a bank's own funds, or funds deposited with it by its customers. The extension of circula-

19

tion credit makes available to borrowers newly created funds which do not decrease or restrict the funds available to anyone else as in the case of commodity credit (q.v.). See also "Credit expansion" and "Monetary theory of the trade cycle."

HA. 433-434, 571-575; M. 264-275.

Circumlocution. The use of indirect or roundabout language. The use of more words than necessary as a means of avoiding a simple direct expression.

Circumscribe. Restrain by drawing a line around; limit or restrict actions to a small area within narrow boundaries.

Civil War, American (1861-1865). The war between the more populous Northern States, known as the Union or the Federals, and the emotionally aroused, secessionist Southern States, known as the Confederate States or the Rebels. The basic issues were slavery, State sovereignty or "States' Rights" and protectionism for industry. Economic factors gave victory to the Union. The North developed great diversified industrial strength, fed itself and blockaded Southern ports. The South, long dependent on cotton and tobacco, lacked food, industry and transportation facilities for keeping her armed forces supplied. The blockade made cotton almost worthless within the Confederacy, while world prices, in terms of gold, shot up to more than ten times prewar prices, causing great distress among English textile workers.

Classical economics. The first comprehensive system of economic theory, first expounded by Adam Smith (1723-1790) in his *Wealth of Nations* (1776). It also included the writings of Jeremy Bentham (1748-1832), David Ricardo (1772-1823), Jean Baptiste Say (1767-1832), Thos. R. Malthus (1766-1834), James Mill (1773-1836), John Stuart Mill (1806-1873) and many others of that era. While not advocates of complete *laissez faire,* this school of economics generally supported the principle that both individuals and society prosper most with a minimum of political intervention. They defended private property, voluntary social cooperation, economic freedom and popular government and provided some of the first basic principles upon which modern economics has been built. Their great weakness was their failure to solve the paradox of value and thus much of their reasoning was based on the labor (objective) theory of value.

HA. 162-164, 175, 231, 653, et al.; also PLG. 29-31, 35, 76.

Classical liberalism. The doctrines and policies of the traditional "liberal" (q.v.).

Classical theory of value. The value theory of Adam Smith (1723-1790), David Ricardo (1772-1823) and their followers, also accepted by Karl Marx (1818-1883). This theory holds that market values are determined by the quantity of labor required to produce what is offered for sale. As later developed, the quality of the labor needed was also taken into consideration.

Coadjuvancy. Mutually helpful assistance.

Cockaigne, Land of, (French). Literally, land of cakes. An imaginary country of idleness and luxury. In Cockaigne the rivers were of wine, houses were built of cakes, the streets were paved with pastry and the stores were filled with free goods. Roasted fowl flew about ready for the eating.
EP. 79; PF. 116, 177.

Coefficient of correlation. A mathematical figure for showing the degree of agreement or uniformity of relationship between two things, groups, sets of facts or series of data or certain qualities thereof. A perfect agreement or uniformity of relationship is unity, or one. Consequently, the nearer the coefficient of correlation is to one, the closer is the agreement or uniformity of relationship for the two matters under consideration.

Cognition. The mental act, process or product of such act or process of knowing, learning, perceiving or of becoming aware.
HA. 647.

Collateral. In business, property, or legal title thereto, which is deposited as security to guarantee the performance of a contract, usually the repayment of a loan.

Coloni, (Latin). Tenant farmers, later serfs who farmed.

Commodity credit. The exchange of a lender's present goods or money for the borrower's promise of payment in future goods or money in which the immediate sacrifice of the lender corresponds exactly to the goods or sum of money received by the borrower. In the case of banks, commodity credit represents loans of banknotes or the extension of demand deposit credit for which the

21

bank holds 100% monetary reserves. In short, the lender forfeits for a time the use or consumption of real wealth which has been transferred to the borrower. Commodity credit contrasts with circulation credit (q.v.).

HA. 433-434; M. 264-265.

Commodity money. A physical commodity originally valued for its commercial uses which has come to be used as money. As long as it remains a commercial commodity, its value as a commodity and as money is interchangeable and dependent on market conditions, i.e., the money relation (q.v.), the demand for it as a commodity and the cost of production (or mining). Modern example: gold.

HA. 428-429; M. 59-67, 482-483.

Communism. See "Socialism" with which communism is synonymous in terms of their common final goal, the public ownership (control) of the means of production and the public management of all production and allocation of finished goods and services. Following the Bolshevist Revolution (1917), the Bolshevist leader, Lenin (1870-1924), chose the name Communist Party for all those dedicated to the use of violence, revolution and civil war to attain their final goal, to distinguish his followers from the socialists, or social democrats who sought the same final goal by democratic processes. In 1928, when it became evident that the Communist Revolution had not eliminated the poverty of the Russian masses, the Communist International proclaimed a material distinction between communism and socialism. It reserved the term "communism" for what Karl Marx (1818-1883), in his *Critique of the Gotha Program* (1875), called the "higher phase of communist society." It would follow socialism when the increase in wealth from socialism would permit an allocation of goods and services on the basis of "From each according to his abilities, to each according to his needs!"

AC. 63-66, 111-112; PF. 140-143; S. 543-553.

Communist International. The international organization whose members are the Communist Parties of all nations having one. It first met at Moscow in 1919 and is also known as the Comintern or the "Third International." Its headquarters are in Moscow and it is the main organization through which the leaders of the Soviet Union seek to convert the rest of the world to the ideology of

"Socialism of the Russian pattern" (q.v.). For its historical antecedents, see "Second International."
S. 550, 552.

Communist Manifesto. In November 1847, the Communist League, a newly formed international group, commissioned Karl Marx (1818-1883) and Friedrich Engels (1820-1895) to draw up a party platform or program for the League. Originally written in German, it appeared on the eve of the 1848 European revolutions which the authors apparently looked upon as the dawn of a communist era. As the best known piece of socialist literature, it has formed the basis of many anticapitalistic movements and should be read for an understanding of the increasing acceptance of the principles of interventionism and socialism during the last century.
AC. 41-42, 63-66, 72, 111; B. 98; OG, 51, 151, 178; PF. 95-101, 103, 141, 175, 184; S. 543.

Comparative cost, law or theory of. The theory of David Ricardo (1772-1823), also known as the Ricardian Law of Association, which holds that when one person, group or nation is superior to another in the production of all goods, it is advantageous for all parties if the more efficient or better endowed producer concentrates on the production of those goods he can produce with the greatest relative superiority and the less effective producer concentrates on those goods he can produce with the least relative deficiency.
HA. 159-164.

Concatenation. State or condition of the correlated action of mutually interdependent processes. Situation where a number of distinct processes mesh or link together with a resulting cumulative effect in a well coordinated movement. A good example of concatenation is the market process wherein the independent value judgments of all potential participants are simultaneously correlated or meshed together to produce market prices which allocate available supplies of economic goods and services. See *Human Action*, paragraph starting on the last line of page 652.

Conceptual realism. The theory that abstract universals, unobservable general classes or ideal types (q.v.) have a reality that is independent, equal and sometimes superior to the reality of their individual parts or specific examples. For instance, conceptual

23

realists consider the abstract term "capital" as something real concrete and permanent with different uses and characteristics from those of the "capital goods" of which it consists. Another example would be "national income." The philosopher A. N. Whitehead (1861-1947) called this the "fallacy of misplaced concreteness."

HA. 45, 145, 515. See also F. A. Hayek's *The Counter-Revolution of Science* (Glencoe, Ill.: Free Press, 1952), p. 54.

Confederates. Name given to the soldiers and citizens of the Confederate States of America, the Southern States of the United States during the Civil War (q.v.).

Congener. A person or thing of the same origin, nature or innate character.

Congeneric. Allied in origin and nature.

Congress of Paris (1856). Representatives of England, France, Austria, Sardinia, Turkey and Russia met for more than a month to draw up and sign the Treaty of Paris (1856), a peace treaty ending the Crimean War. The provisions affecting naval warfare included: (1) Abolition of wartime privateers; (2) Guarantee of safe passage for all enemy property, except war contraband, carried on neutral ships; (3) Guarantee of safety to all shipping on the Danube River; (4) Provision that all blockades must be effective in order to be binding on neutral shipping; (5) Black Sea opened up for the first time to commercial shipping of all nations; (6) Ban placed on all naval ships in the Black Sea and on any arsenals or fortifications on Black Sea coastal areas.

Congruity. State or quality of being appropriately adapted, suitably consistent or harmoniously related.

Conquistadors, (from the Spanish). Name given to the sixteenth century Spanish conquerors of Mexico and Peru. The two best known Conquistadors were Hernán Cortés (1485-1547) who conquered Mexico and Francisco Pizarro (1470?-1541) who operated in Peru and founded Lima.

Continental currency. The paper notes issued by the Continental Congress to help finance the American Revolution. They entitled the bearer to receive "Spanish milled dollars, or the value thereof in gold or silver" but were never so redeemed. The original issue of $2,000,000 was authorized on June 22, 1775. By the end of 1779, the total issued reached $241,522,280. Two years later they were worthless. In 1790, after they had been out of circulation for almost ten years, the new government agreed to redeem them at one new dollar for every 40 continental dollars, but only six or seven million were ever presented for redemption.

Contracyclical policies. Interventionist policies which the sponsors hope will counteract the undesired but inevitable effects of credit expansion (q.v.). At best, such policies merely postpone the day of reckoning. See "Trade cycle" and "Monetary theory of the trade cycle."

HA. 798-800.

Contradictio in adjecto, (Latin). A logical inconsistency between a noun and its modifying adjective. Examples are "square circle," "inert activity" and "controlled or non-market prices."

Coolies. The lowest paid unskilled laborers of, or from, China, India or other highly populated Asiatic areas.

Copulation. The act of sexual intercourse.

Corn-hog cycle. A large corn crop results in lower corn prices, causing farmers to increase their breeding and feeding of pigs which, when they mature and are sold as hogs, depress hog prices. Farmers then reduce their production of hogs which in turn reduces the demand for corn and thus the price of corn, and the cycle is then ready to repeat itself.

Corn Laws. British laws for the regulation of the grain trade from 1436 to 1846. In the later years, from about 1790, it became increasingly evident that these laws were primarily protecting the British land owners from foreign competition and thus raising the prices of bread and cereals, the basic diet of industrial workers. In 1838, the Anti-Corn Law League was founded in Manchester, England. The League, led by Richard Cobden (1804-1865), "The Apostle of Free Trade," and John Bright (1811-1889), was largely responsible for the repeal of the Corn Law in 1846 and the growing acceptance of the *laissez faire* principles of the Manchester School (q.v.). NOTE: Corn is the name generally given to the leading cereal grass consumed as food by a country's inhabitants. In England, corn is what Americans know as wheat.

25

In Scotland and Ireland, corn is oats, while on the European continent, corn is usually what Americans know as rye.

Corporativism. The economic program of the Italian Fascist Party, largely copying the program of British "guild socialism" (q.v.). All organized economic activities were divided into 22 sectors, each of which was represented by a corporation. The council of each corporation was presided over by a Fascist Party member and was comprised of government appointed "experts" and representatives of employees, employers and the Fascist Party. Each council was responsible to the Minister of Corporations for the management of its corporation, and its members were also members of the Chamber of Fasces and Corporations, which was scheduled to become the lower house of the legislature. In practice, the Corporation council members merely ratified the decisions of the nation's Fascist dictator, Benito Mussolini (1883-1945). S. 576-577.

Corporazione, (Italian). Corporation, guild, association. S. 577.

Corvée, (French). A feudal term for the forced unpaid labor a peasant performed for his lord or vassal. The term was later applied to such labor that inhabitants must perform under the direction of the public authorities, being a type of tax in the form of forced labor.

Cosmogony. A theory or account of the creation and development of the world or universe.

Cosmology. A general science or theory which describes or explains the extent and orderly structure of the universe, with emphasis on the nature of its parts as well as the laws, processes and relationships by which the parts are coordinated in time and space. Also a specific theory, body of doctrine or school of thought which deals with or relates to the natural order of the universe.

Cost. (1) Whatever asset must be spent, foregone, given up or otherwise sacrificed; or (2) Whatever liability must be acquired or suffered in order to obtain or produce something or attain some end. A cost may be a matter of money, labor, lives, time, trouble, pain, debt or anything else that men value and take into consideration when deciding to seek a specific goal or good. The contemplation of a cost is always a judgment of value (q.v.). Any cost expressed in monetary terms is a price, i.e., a quantity of money.

Counterpoise.   Offset; balance; counterbalance; act as an equal effect.

Crack-up boom.   The final short-lived boom that occurs in the last stages of a seemingly endless inflation. The crack-up boom results from a "flight into goods or real values" (q.v.) and marks the end of an inflation by a complete breakdown of the monetary system.

HA. 427-428, 436, 469, 555, 562; M. 227-230.

Credit contraction.   Reduction in outstanding circulation credit (q.v.); reversal of a prior credit expansion (q.v.). NOTE: Credit contraction has no reference to a reduction in commodity credit (q.v).

Credit expansion.   An increase in the quantity of monetary units created by an increase in bank loans over and above the number of monetary units that savers have released to the banks for lending to third parties. In short, monetary loans in excess of monetary savings available for lending. Credit expansion is only possible with a fractional reserve banking system. Other things remaining the same, every credit expansion must create a boom or upswing in economic activity. This boom can only be sustained by a continued credit expansion at an ever accelerated rate sufficient to induce a repetition of the same activities at the increased prices resulting from the previous credit expansions. See "Circulation credit" and "Monetary theory of the trade cycle."

B. 84; HA. 434, 440-444, 554-557, 570-571, 793-798; OG. 251-254; PF. 58-61, 68-69, 102, 150-161; S. 531; also PLG. 179-181, 187-195.

Credit money.   Non-commodity money which consists of non-interest bearing claims that are not redeemable on demand. Usually, credit money is money that was originally issued as a redeemable money-substitute but whose redemption was later suspended either indefinitely or until some future date. It retains value because it has general acceptance as a medium of exchange. Credit money is "money in both the broader and narrower senses" (q.v.).

27

HA. 429; M. 61-62, 482- 483.

Currency.   Anything which passes from person to person and is commonly acceptable as a medium of exchange (q.v.).

Currency School.   This British group originated from the writings of David Ricardo (1772-1823) in opposition to the Banking School (q.v.). The Currency School advocated the "currency doctrine" in the nineteenth century controversy over the laws which should govern the Bank of England and form the basis of the British monetary system. The "currency doctrine" maintains that all future changes in the nation's quantity of money should correspond precisely with changes in the nation's holdings of monetary metal (after 1853, gold only). In general, the Currency School opposed free banking principles and the legal sanction for any discretionary increases or decreases in the nation's quantity of money, which, in their opinion, included banknotes but not demand deposits subject to transfer or withdrawal by check. In short, the School opposed the practice of issuing fiduciary banknotes against commercial paper and government securities and sought a legal ban on the issue of any new banknotes except against 100% gold reserves.

The Currency School was successful in incorporating its ideas into the Bank (Peel's) Act of 1844 (q.v.). However, this Act, while prohibiting further fiduciary issues of banknotes, permitted a great expansion of circulation credit (q.v.) in the form of demand deposits. Consequently, the Act failed to limit the increase in fiduciary media as the Currency School had anticipated.

Because no short definition can be fully satisfactory, the reader is urged to read the references.

HA. 438-444, 571-572; M. 343-345, 367-373; PF. 67. See also J. Laurence Laughlin's *The Principles of Money* (N.Y.: Chas. Scribner's Sons, 1903/1926), pp. 238-281; and Lloyd W. Mints' *A History of Banking Theory, in Great Britain and the United States* (Univ. of Chicago Press, 1945), pp. 74-124.

Customs duties, customs.   Taxes levied or collected on imports or exports.

Cyclical movements of trade.   See "Trade cycle."

28

D

Daimios, (Japanese). The chief feudal barons of a territory in Japan. While vassals of the Mikado (Emperor), they exercised independent authority in their baronies. They lost their power (1868) in the changes that followed from the opening of Japan to Western contacts and ideas.

Damocles, Sword of. See "Sword of Damocles."

Daphnis and Chloë. One of the earliest romantic novels known. It describes how two naive children of rural herders grew up as lovers and overcame severe obstacles to achieve a happy married life in the country. The original manuscript was by a Greek Sophist, Longus (circa 300 A.D.). A French version by Jacques Amyot (1513-1593) appeared in 1559 and in 1810, Paul Louis Courier (1772-1825) found the original manuscript in a Florence, Italy, library and republished it.

Darwinism, social or sociological. A distortion of the doctrine of Charles Darwin (1809-1882) that the evolution and improvement of mankind is the result of a constant struggle for existence against environmental conditions into a quite different doctrine that the evolution and improvement of mankind is the result of constant wars, civil strife and revolutions whereby physically superior men vanquish the physically inferior.
OG. 120-122.

Das Kapital. The main work of the socialist, Karl Marx (1818-1883); a poorly written, voluminous, three volume anti-capitalistic dissertation based on the classical (or labor) theory of value. The rough draft of the three volumes was completed in 1865. Volume

I appeared in 1867. Volumes II and III were promised the printer at six month intervals. When Volume I failed to attract notable attention, Marx stopped his finishing touches on the other volumes. After his death, 16 years later, his collaborator and financial backer, Friedrich Engels (1820-1895) brought out Volume II in 1885, and Volume III in 1894. *Das Kapital* is a book that is much more often quoted and referred to than really read or studied. See "Marxism."

For a critique from the Austrian viewpoint, see "Unresolved Contradiction in the Marxian Economic System" written in 1896 by Eugen von Böhm-Bawerk (1851-1914) and appearing in Volume I of *Shorter Classics of Böhm-Bawerk* (South Holland, Ill.: Libertarian Press, 1961), earlier editions under the title "Karl Marx and the Close of His System" (Macmillan Co., 1898, and Augustus M. Kelley, 1949). See also Böhm-Bawerk's *Capital and Interest* (South Holland, Ill.: Libertarian Press, 1959), particularly Volume I, Chapter XII, "The Exploitation Theory," which has also been printed as a separate extract.

See also PLG. 31-39, 49, 109, 116-117, 175, 288.

Das spezifische Verstehen der Geisteswissenschaften, (German). The specific understanding of the moral sciences. See "Understanding." NOTE: *"Geisteswissenschaften"* was introduced into the German language for the term, "moral sciences," as used by the English economist, John Stuart Mill (1806-1873).

Declaration of Independence (July 4, 1776). The document, signed by representatives of the thirteen American colonies assembled in Philadelphia, Pennsylvania, in the Second Continental Congress, which declares the independence of the United States from England. It proclaims that governments are instituted among men to secure the unalienable rights of men to life, liberty and the pursuit of happiness, and to that end, the signers pledged their lives, fortunes and sacred honor.

OG. 79.

Deduction, n. deductive, adj.   In logic, reasoning from a general (or universal) premise, that is either assumed or known to be true, to an individual or particular instance of that generality. Example: All men act in an attempt to improve their situation; therefore,

Mary's act was an attempt to improve her situation. The derived conclusion is always implicit in the original premise and is necessarily as correct as that original premise. The economics propounded by the Austrian School (q.v.) has been entirely developed on the basis of deductive reasoning.

HA. 38-41; UF. 21-27, 44-45.

De facto, (Latin).   In fact; actually; in reality.

Deflation.   In popular nonscientific usage, a large decrease in the quantity of "money in the broader sense" (q.v.) which results in a rise in the purchasing power of the monetary unit, falsifies economic calculation and impairs the value of accounting as a means of appraising profits and losses. Deflation affects the various prices, wage rates and interest rates at different times and to different extents. It thus disarranges consumption, investment, the course of production and the structure of business and industry while increasing the wealth and income of some and decreasing that of others. Deflation does not alter the available quantity of consumable wealth. It merely removes a quantity of monetary units from the market, thus permitting each of the remaining units to command a higher purchasing power.

This popular definition, a large decrease in the quantity of money, is satisfactory for history and politics but it lacks the precision of a scientific term since the distinction between a small decrease and a large decrease in the quantity of money and the differences in their effects are merely a matter of degree.

A more precise concept for use in theoretical analysis is any decrease in the quantity of money in the broader sense which is not offset by a corresponding decrease in the need for money in the broader sense, so that a rise in the objective exchange-value (purchasing power) of money must ensue.

See PLG. 234-237.

Deism.   In the eighteenth century sense, Deism meant a belief in one God as the Creator of the world or universe and opposition to revelation and the thought that God dwelt in man and was continuously active in the affairs of man and the world. Deists aimed at what they considered a rational as opposed to a mysterious faith. This led them to "naturalistic" explanations of religion and a belief in eternal "natural laws" which were regarded as the will of God.

De jure, (Latin). By law; legally; by right as opposed to *de facto,* in fact.

De lege ferenda, (Latin). For proposing or making a law.

De lege lata, (Latin). From existing law.

Demand deposit. Money placed in or credited to a commercial bank account which the depositor is legally entitled to withdraw on demand without prior notice. In practice, most withdrawals are in the form of checks which merely transfer sums within the banking system. Demand deposits are also known as deposit currency or checkbook money.

H. 432.

Deposit currency. The demand deposit liabilities of banks. The total amount held in bank accounts subject to immediate withdrawal or transfer to another account upon presentation of a check duly signed by the owner of such a bank account. Sometimes referred to as checkbook money. Like banknotes, deposit currency is a money-substitute (q.v.) and "money in the broader sense" (q.v.). Only the monetary reserves held against their withdrawal are "money in the narrower sense" (q.v.). The amount of deposit currency in excess of the reserves held against withdrawal is "fiduciary media" (q.v.).

HA. 432-448, 571; M. 52-59, 268-275, 278-280, 319-321, 482-483.

Depression. In the trade cycle (q.v.), the period of economic readjustment which inevitably follows a boom created by inflation or credit expansion. The characteristics of a depression period are greatly reduced business activity, mass unemployment and much human misery. These characteristics continue until the illusions of the boom have been dispelled and economic activity has readjusted to the realities of the existing conditions. Attempts to interfere with free and flexible prices, wage and interest rates prevent recovery and prolong the depression period. See "Monetary theory of the trade cycle."

AC. 60-61; HA. 563, 575-578; PF. 103; also PLG. 175-231.

Deproletarianization. An improvement in the living conditions of the manual workers that raises their standard of living to the customary standards of the "middle classes."

Deus ex machina, (Latin). Literally, a god out of a machine, from the ancient theatrical practice of using a machine to produce on stage a god capable of solving problems human beings are unable to solve. Hence, reliance on providential intervention or other unspecified means for the solution of an otherwise unsolvable human problem.

Dialectical materialism. A Marxian concept developed out of a combination of Hegelian dialectics and the materialist philosophy of Ludwig von Feuerbach (1804-1872). It holds that the inherent logic of the "material productive forces" (q.v.) propel society via the class struggle toward socialism "with the inexorability of a law of nature." See also "Materialism," sense 2.
HA. 79-84; TH. 102-158; UF. 30-33.

Dialectics. A philosophical term applied to methods of debate or argumentation that seek to prove or disprove the truth of something by the rules of logic or the laws of reasoning.

Dictionnaire philosophique, (French). Philosophical dictionary, title of a work by Voltaire (François Marie Arouet, 1694-1778), a French writer and philosopher.

Didactic. Instructive; educational; fitted or intended to teach.

Differential equations. Complicated equations which express certain formulas of constant relationships and in which changes in the value or magnitude assigned to certain variable factors determine the value or magnitude of the other variable factors. These equations are helpful in solving many problems of higher mathematics and the natural sciences because the knowledge of certain known factors permits one to compute the value or magnitude of the unknown variable factors. Such equations are of no help in solving problems of human action (economics) because there is no certainty of constant relationships between the values of different factors. See "Mathematical economics" and "Marginal theory of value."
HA. 710-715.

33

Dilettantism. The quality characteristics of one who pursues an art, occupation or branch of knowledge superficially as a pastime or amusement without acquiring skill or proficiency.

Diminishing returns, law of. See "Returns, law of," of which it is a part.

Direct exchange. The trading of goods for goods (barter), goods for services ("truck system"), or services of one kind for services of another kind without the intermediary use of money or any other medium of exchange. Direct exchange contrasts with indirect exchange which involves the use of a medium of exchange, usually money, in a two step process of sale and purchase in order to obtain the desired goods or services.

Discount, rate of. An interest rate calculated and payable in advance. Unless otherwise specified or suggested, the term refers to the official rate charged by the central bank for discounting the short term paper and other eligible investments of other banks. In the United States, the official discount rate is the rate the Federal Reserve Banks charge their member banks. In Great Britain, the discount rate of the Bank of England is known as the bank rate.

Discursive reasoning. Thinking a problem through logically step by step from one premise to another in an attempt to arrive at an acceptable conclusion or explanation, as opposed to intuitive knowledge.

Disparate. Utterly unlike or different; essentially distinct or dissimilar; incapable of being compared.

Disquisition. A complete or systematic study or investigation; a formal essay, treatise, discussion or dissertation.

Disutility. The state or quality of being contrary to one's desires or well-being. The state or quality of producing undesirable conditions, such as those of annoyance, discomfort, irritation, uneasiness, pain, suffering or distress. The opposite or negative of utility.

Disutility of labor. The discomfort, uneasiness, inconvenience or

34

pain inherent in human effort. Because of this quality men regard labor as a burden and prefer leisure to toil or labor.

HA. 65, 131-138, 611-617.

Doctrinaire, n. and adj.   One who is dogmatic, impractical, visionary and uninterested in views differing from his own.

Dogma.   A concept or principle accepted as absolute truth on the basis of unquestioned acceptance of an authority's statement to that effect rather than on the basis of logical reasoning or demonstrated proof.

Do ut des, (Latin).   "I give as you give," or "I give that you may give."

Duopoly, duopolist.   Literally, two sellers. A market situation in which two individuals or business organizations own or control the total supply of a given commodity or service. A duopolist is one of the two who own or control such a total supply.

HA. 363-364.

E

Easy money. A loan market condition in which funds can be borrowed at lower interest rates than those that would prevail under free market conditions. Easy money policies lead to an expansion of circulation credit (q.v.) in that more funds are made available in the form of loans than savers have accumulated and set aside for that purpose.

Eclecticism. The policy, or advocacy of a policy, of constructing a composite system of thought or ideology by selecting different parts from different existing systems of thought or ideologies. In the case of economics, a science of thoroughly integrated and interdependent parts, this practice must result in policies, or the advocacy of policies, which, when properly analyzed, will be found to contain untenable contradictions and inconsistencies.

Econometrics. The attempts of statisticians and mathematicians to discover economic laws and solve problems of human action by the use of statistical data which necessarily relate to the past. Econometricians maintain that science is measurement and assume both a constancy and regularity in economic data that permits them to use precise mathematical measurement for testing and developing economic theory.

Actually, the only measurable magnitudes of human action are those related to historical facts. The ideas and value judgments which determine human participation in the market process are neither constant nor certain. All future human actions are thus uncertain variables which are incapable of either quantification or measurement. Consequently, the use of mathematics, as a means for determining economic theory applicable to future human actions, is futile.

HA. 350-357; UF. 4, 62-63.

Economia politica e corporativa, (Italian). Literally, political and corporate (or corporativist) economy. Actually, the doctrine of Italian corporativism (q.v.) as taught at the Italian Universities under the regime of Fascism (q.v.).

Economic man. A concept developed by the nineteenth century epigones (q.v.) of British Classical Political Economy. It depicts man as if he were solely and constantly motivated by a desire for monetary gain to the exclusion of all other human desires. It is thus an attempt by these epigones to explain and justify the pre-occupation of classical economics (q.v.) with the activities of businessmen and their neglect to pay sufficient attention to the activities of consumers.

EP. 179-181; HA. 62-64, 239-240, 651.

Economic problem, the. How to employ the available means in such a way that no want more urgently felt should remain unsatisfied because the means suitable for its attainment were employed for the attainment of a want less urgently felt, i.e., wasted.

HA. 207; also PLG. 15-16, 68-69.

Economics. A theoretical science which provides a comprehension of the meaning and relevance of purposive (conscious) human actions. It is not about things and material objects; it is about the meanings and actions of men. Economics is a science of the means men must select if they are to attain their humanly attainable ends which they have chosen in accordance with their value judgments. However, the valuation and selection of ends are beyond the scope of economics and every other science. Economics enables men to predict the "qualitative" effects to be expected from the adoption of specific measures or economic policies, but such predictions cannot be "quantitative" as there are no constant relations in the valuations which determine, guide and alter human actions.

For Mises' comments "On Some Popular Errors Concerning the Scope and Method of Economics," including Macroeconomics, see Chapter 5 of *The Ultimate Foundation of Economic Science.*

HA. 1-3, 6-10, 64-69, 92-93, 647-648, 651, 653-654; TH. 203; UF. 67-69, 73; also PLG. 1-20, 23.

Egalitarianism. Equalitarianism; the untenable belief that all men are biologically equal and that all inequalities in income, wealth and opportunity are the results of unscrupulous usurpation and expropriation of the masses by the capitalists. Egalitarians contend that governments should use their coercive powers to restore and maintain the equality with which all men are supposed to be born.

TH. 528, *et al.*

Ego, (Latin).   Self; an individual's inner or mental consciousness. In psychoanalysis, the term applied to that part of the structure of the human mind from which conscious urges and desires arise.

Élan vital, (French).   The urge or impulse that is an essential part of all human life; the fundamental source of human action. Term used by the philosopher, Henri Bergson (1859-1941), for the source of efficient causation and evolution of human life that passes from generation to generation.

Elasticity of demand.   The extent to which the demand for goods or services is expected to react in response to changes in the prices or wages for such goods or services.

Electors.   The high German princes who were entitled to vote in the elections of new King-Emperors of the Holy Roman (German) Empire from about 1257 to 1806. Originally seven in number, and never more than nine, they also formed the top college of the three-college Imperial Diet or Reichstag, the other two consisting of (1) lesser lay and spiritual princes, and (2) representatives of the towns.

Elysium, (from Greek mythology).   Elysian Fields; the dwelling place of all noble and virtuous persons after they have departed from this earth. It is a place where the inhabitants are presumed to enjoy eternal bliss, the highest kind of happiness.

Empathy.   The ability to experience sympathetically the emotions of another; the emotional penetration of another person, frequently used in connection with the creator of a work of art.

Empirical.   Depending on the existence of a regularity in the causality and succession of natural events which permits the acquisition of human knowledge from experiments or experience because identical natural or physical conditions and events always produce identical results or consequences. The natural sciences are empirical. The social or human sciences are not.

UF. 21, 27, 63, *et al.*

Empiricism. The theory that the only source of human knowledge is experience. Empiricism assumes a regularity in the flow of events and proclaims that experiments and observation are the main instruments for the acquisition of knowledge.

UF. 21, 27.

Enclosure movement. Under England's feudal system, most of the rural area consisted of open fields and forests with large sections set aside for workers to raise their own grain and graze livestock. With the rise of the cottage industry, private employment and both agricultural and industrial production for the market instead of the manor, more and more of the open fields (commons) were enclosed with fences for the exclusive use of their owners, usually the landed aristocracy, while many of the smaller holdings were consolidated into large ones. The movement required many Acts of Parliament and extended over the eighteenth and most of the nineteenth centuries. The lower classes were opposed to the movement. It resulted in an increase in agricultural production and the creation of a rural proletariat which then formed the labor force of the developing British manufacturing in the "Industrial Revolution" (q.v.).

English Revolution of 1688. See "Revolution of 1688, English."

Enlightenment, the. See "Age of Enlightenment."

Entbehrung, (German). Privation; abstinence; frugality.

Entrepreneur, (French). Literally, undertaker. In general usage, an entrepreneur is a businessman, one who plans, organizes and directs, i.e., undertakes, a business enterprise, primarily for his own gain or loss. In scientific economic theory, entrepreneur means acting man in the sense of the uncertainty inherent in every action, in that all human actions are undertaken in the flux of time and thus involve speculation in the anticipation of future events. The entrepreneur attempts to act so as to produce a more desirable future situation than he anticipates would result from either no action or any other possible action on his part. The entrepreneur, i.e., the acting man, is the one to whom the profits or losses of an action first redound.

AC. 64, 100, 107; B. 29, 100; HA. 252-256, 291-300, 649; PF. 111, 117, 146; also PLG. 67, 114-115.

Entrepreneurial component of interest rate. See "Interest rate, entrepreneurial component."

Entrepreneurial profit and loss. Profit or loss from market transactions calculated in monetary units. An increase (profit) or decrease (loss) in the estimated monetary equivalent of the net assets (total assets minus total liabilities) of an individual or business unit over a specified period of time or resulting from specified business transactions. Entrepreneurial profits result from a better-than-others ability to anticipate and satisfy market demands. This is done by directing the use or combination of the factors of production available on the market in such a way that the goods or services produced bring a higher market price than other products made with the same factors of production.

Entrepreneurial profits and losses emerge due to the following ever present market factors: (1) The uncertainty of future consumer demand; (2) The ceaseless changes in the demand for and supply of the various human and physical factors of production, which constantly create new opportunities for better adjusting production to anticipated future consumer wants; (3) The fact that all production takes time; and (4) Differences in entrepreneurial ability to foresee, at the time production must start, what the most urgent wants of consumers will be at the various future times when the available alternative processes of production might be completed.

Entrepreneurial profits and losses are society's appraisal of the contributions of individuals and other business units to societal welfare or satisfaction. Entrepreneurial profits and losses are the means that consumers use to shift the control of capital, and the direction of production, into the hands of those who have demonstrated their ability to serve consumers best.

AC. 86; B. 20-39; HA. 212-214, 289-300; PF. 108-150.

Entropy. The mathematical measure of the unavailable energy in a thermo-dynamic problem concerning the transfer of heat into mechanical energy or vice versa at a given temperature.

Epicureanism. The Greek school of thought founded by Epicurus (342-270 B.C.) that held that the joys of the mind are superior to the pleasures of the body.

Epigone. A follower, adherent or disciple, often with connotations of following in time and of lesser importance than the master or masters.

Epistemology, n. **epistemological,** adj. The theory of human knowledge; the basis of the sciences of man which is concerned with the origin, structure, methods and validity of human knowledge. It deals with the mental phenomena of human life: thinking, perceiving and knowing. It assumes that the logical structure of the human mind is unchanging.

UF. 1-2.

Equation of exchange. An equation, first made popular by Irving Fisher (1867-1947) in his *Purchasing Power of Money* (1911), which states: The average amount of money outstanding (M) multiplied by velocity (V), i.e., total expenditures divided by the average amount of money outstanding, equals the sum of the average price paid for each good and service (p) multiplied by the quantity of each sold (q), or $MV = \Sigma (pq + p'q' \ldots + p^n q^n)$, or more often $MV = PT$, in which P represents average prices and T the total physical volume of trade.

In short, the equation merely equates the sums spent to the total of prices paid, assuming an equality between the values of the prices paid and the goods bought. This is contrary to the subjective or marginal theory of value, wherein all voluntary exchanges are exchanges of unequal values. In using totals and averages, the equation of exchange also implies the fallacies inherent in the concepts of "price level" and the "neutrality of money" (q.v.).

Although designed as an explanation of the purchasing power of money, the equation of exchange is an holistic concept which fails to explain either how the purchasing power of money arises or how changes in it occur. The purchasing power of money is actually determined by the reactions of individuals to their ever changing individual situations and not by any mathematical formula.

HA. 204, 398-401, 408-416.

Equilibrium. A state or condition where opposing forces or offsetting influences are exactly equal and thus in balance, i.e., a state of rest or inaction. Equilibrium can exist only so long as there are no new data, forces or influences capable of changing or disturbing existing conditions. Equilibrium is thus a state or condition which is impossible of achievement where market conditions or processes are constantly affected by the disturbing element of new human actions. See "Evenly rotating economy" and "Mathematical economics."

Equilibrium price.   A price (quantity of money) at which there are no further sales because supply and demand are in balance.

Equity capital.   Investments in the form of ownership titles, usually shares of capital stock, as distinguished from investments in loans, bonds or other forms of debt which represent claims which must be met and fully satisfied before any claims, dividends or other distributions to the owners or shareholders.

Equivocation.   Use of a word or expression, open to more than one meaning, so as to mislead or confuse, either because the user intends to mislead or is himself confused. In a discussion or argument, the repetition of a basic term in another sense than that in which it was originally used.

Ergastulum, (Latin).   The compound of ancient Roman villas and farms in which the slaves were kept when not working in the fields.

Ersatz, (German).   Substitute. As a rule, the term implies that the Ersatz is inferior to the article for which it is a substitute.
   B. 24.

Esoteric.   Exclusive; restricted; erudite. The term implies being limited to specialists or an exclusive inner circle by a quality of being too complex, scholarly or profound for popular dissemination or understanding.

Esprit de corps, (French).   Literally, "spirit of the body." Special spirit of a group or organized body implying exceptional loyalty, devotion or enthusiasm of the members for the cause for which the group was formed.

Étatist, n. and adj., (French).   Statist, in the sense of an advocate of, or tendency toward, the concentration of all economic controls and planning in the hands of the government. See "Statism."

Étatism appears in two forms: socialism and interventionism. Both have in common the goal of subordinating the individual unconditionally to the state, the social apparatus of compulsion and coercion.

OG. 5-11, 44-111, 267-271, 285-286.

États-Généraux, (French).   States-General, an early French assembly of representatives. It first met in 1302 and met irregularly until 1789 at the call of the King. It consisted of the representatives of the three main *États,* the high clergy, the high nobility and the Third Estate (q.v.). Its chief function was to approve the King's revenue proposals.

Ethnology.   The science concerned with the origin, development, distinguishing characteristics and geographical distribution of human races.

Euclidian geometry.   Geometry as first propounded in the axioms of Euclid about 300 B.C. Euclidian geometry is based on the concept of flat and endless space, as opposed to the concept of curved space, as used in plotting the longitudes of a spherical body. In the flat space concept, parallel longitudinal lines never meet as they eventually must in projections on the exterior of a sphere, as the earth's longitudes do at the North and South Poles.

Eudaemonism.   The theory that the final goal of all human action is happiness.

EP. 150.

Euphemistic.   Pertaining to, or characterized by, the use of a pleasant sounding word or expression with agreeable connotations in place of a plainer, more accurate one, the meaning of which might be offensive, unpleasant or embarrassing.

Evanescent.   Fleeting; transient; likely to vanish or disappear momentarily.

Evenly rotating economy.   An imaginary economy in which all transactions and physical conditions are repeated without change in each similar cycle of time. Everything is imagined to continue exactly as before, including all human ideas and goals. Under such fictitious constant repetitive conditions, there can be no net change in any supply or demand and therefore there cannot be any changes in prices. The evenly rotating economy is a helpful device for studying the logical effects produced by the introduction of particular individual changes.

HA. 246-250; PF. 119, 147-148; UF. 42.

Ex definitione, (Latin). By definition.

Exegesis. Exposition, interpretation or explanation of a text; an elaboration on the significance of an idea or a passage in a written work.

Exorcism. The act or process of driving off an evil spirit by a solemn oath or magic rite.

Expatiate. Discuss without limits or restraint; enlarge upon almost without end.

External costs. Those burdens, damages or other costs of a human action which do not fall on the person or firm responsible for the action. Such costs are often neglected in the economic calculations which determine whether or not an action is or will be considered profitable. An example of an external cost would be the burden or expense of smoke and noise nuisances imposed on neighbors.

HA. 654-661.

External drain. Withdrawal or outflow of gold from a country.

External economies. Those gains, benefits or other advantages of a human action which necessarily go to a person or firm that does not participate in the action. Such advantageous results are often neglected in the economic calculations which determine whether or not an action is or will be considered profitable. An example of such an incidental benefit would be the gain A's neighbors reap from a fence built by A on their boundary lines.

HA. 654-663.

Extirpation. Total destruction by the rooting out or elimination of the cause or means of continuing.

Extroversive labor. Human exertion undertaken because one prefers the expected proceeds over and above the satisfaction obtainable from leisure. Extroversive labor contrasts with introversive labor (q.v.) which is human exertion undertaken for the satisfaction the exertions themselves provide. All work undertaken for compensation or for the final product is extroversive labor.

F

Fabianism.   The socialist principles and policies of the Fabian Society founded in 1884 in order to introduce socialism into Great Britain slowly and slyly. The Society was named after the Roman general Quintus Fabius Maximus (died 203 B.C.) who avoided open and decisive confrontation with his opponents while wearing them down with delaying tactics, misleading maneuvers and continuous harassment. Prominent Fabians included Sidney and Beatrice Webb (1859-1947, 1858-1943), Bernard Shaw (1856-1950) and Harold J. Laski (1893-1950).

PF. 61.

Factor of production.   A human service or material good that can be used to contribute to the success of a process of production. A constituent element of any production process. Examples would be labor, natural resources and capital goods (q.v.). NOTE: Factors of production can be classified as to (1) human (labor) or non-human (material) factors, or (2) original or produced factors. The term "factor of production," as used by Mises, does not include the time factor, although he has referred to time as an "immaterial factor of production."

Failure monopoly.   A monopoly which depends upon the use of a prior malinvestment which it would be clearly unprofitable for anyone to duplicate. An example would be the operation of an already existing exclusive capital structure when consumers will buy the output at prices which exceed operating expenses but which fail to yield the sums which those with uncommitted savings can expect to earn from other investments open to them.

Fait accompli, (French).   Accomplished fact; thing already done.

Fascism, Italian.   The policies and principles of the Fascist Party of Italy providing for the complete regimentation of business and the suppression of all opposition. This Party, founded in 1919 by a former socialist editor, Benito Mussolini (1883-1945), marched on Rome in 1922. Mussolini then assumed control of the government and gradually expanded his power until he became an absolute dictator. After the successful Allied invasion of Italy, the Fascists were deposed in 1943 and Mussolini was assassinated by Italian opponents in 1945.

AC. 97, 109; B. 96, 108; S. 561, 572, 574-578; UF. 130.

Favorable balance of payments.   See "Balance of payments."

Featherbedding.   The labor union practice in a hampered market economy of forcing employers (1) to employ more persons than necessary for the efficient performance of a task, or (2) to pay persons for work they have not performed.

Federal Reserve Act of 1913.   The law creating the Federal Reserve System with its 12 Federal Reserve Banks, which act as the American "Central bank" (q.v.). The Act has been amended many times. The underlying idea was to provide an "elastic currency" through the creation of an American central bank, without arousing the then existing unpopularity of every centralization in the United States and the traditional hostility to the central bank idea due to the experience with two preceding Banks of the United States. See also "Credit expansion," "Depression" and "Monetary theory of the trade cycle."

For helpful critiques of the role of the Federal Reserve System in American economic development, see Benjamin M. Anderson's *Economics and the Public Welfare* (N.Y.: Van Nostrand, 1949), Murray N. Rothbard's *America's Great Depression* (Princeton, N.J.: Van Nostrand, 1963; Los Angeles: Nash, 1972) and PLG, 187-293.

Federal Reserve Notes.   Legal tender notes of the American Federal Reserve System. From 1914 to June 21, 1917, these banknotes were secured by 100% short term rediscounted commercial paper, plus a reserve of not less than 40% in gold. In 1917, the reserve requirements were changed to not less than 40% in gold with the balance to 100% consisting in private and public obligations meeting certain legal requirements. From 1914 to 1933, Federal Reserve notes were redeemable in gold upon presentation. In 1933, their redeemability ceased except for those presented by foreign governments, their central banks and certain international organizations. In 1945, during World War II, the gold reserve requirement was reduced to "not less than 25%." In the 1960's, as the actual gold reserves dropped, there was considerable agitation for the reduction or elimination of this requirement. In 1968, the gold reserve requirement was dropped. Since then they have been secured solely by evidences of private and public debts and have been issuable without limit against such debts. On August 15, 1971, President Nixon suspended their redeemability by foreign governments, their central banks and international organizations. They are now [1974] in effect fiat money (q.v.).

PLG. 188-193.

Feudalism. The social and political order of allegiance, land tenure and military service which gradually developed over large parts of Central and Western Europe after the collapse of the Roman Empire. The land was divided into fiefs or feuds, each with a manor occupied by a vassal or noble (member of the Second Estate) who was beholden for his tenancy to a superior lord, king or emperor to whom he owed tribute and military service. Below each vassal were the subtenants, known as serfs or villeins. Its main characteristic was that all political and military power was vested in the hands of the owners of the land. It slowly disappeared step by step as the modern ages replaced the Middle Ages.

B. 15.

Fiat, (Latin). Literally, let it be done. Order, command, decision, or statute of an authoritative power.

Fiat justitia, ne pereat mundus, (Latin). Let justice be done, (so) the world not be destroyed.

Fiat justitia, pereat mundus, (Latin). Let justice be done, (though) the world be destroyed.

Fiat money. A coin or piece of paper of insignificant commodity

47

value that a government has declared to be money and to which the government has given "legal tender" quality. Fiat money neither represents nor is a claim for commodity money. Fiat money is issued without any set intention to redeem it and consequently no reserves are set aside for that purpose. The value of fiat money rests on the acceptance of political law or fiat. Fiat money is money in both the broader and narrower senses.

HA. 428-430; M. 60-62, 482-483.

Fiduciary media. Money-substitutes freely accepted at face value which consist in claims to payment on demand of specified sums of money in excess of the monetary reserves held for their redemption. Fiduciary money includes token money, bank or treasury notes and demand deposits (deposit currency or checkbook money) which exceed the amount of cash reserves immediately available for their conversion into money proper. Fiduciary media are money-substitutes (q.v.) and "money in the broader sense" (q.v.) but not "money in the narrower sense" (q.v.).

HA. 432-444; M. 52-54, 133; and Part III, particularly 263-297 and 319-339, 482-483.

Final price. In short, the price that would eventually emerge if no new data appeared to change the course of market actions and conditions. The hypothetical or imaginary price which would result with the passage of the time necessary to carry to completion all actions which are the consequence of using existing human knowledge and factors of production in attempts to satisfy presently held value scales in so far as human action can satisfy them. A final price is hypothetical or imaginary because it contemplates no change in human ideas, knowledge or value scales during the time needed to carry out the actions momentarily decided upon at any one time. This implies an actual impossibility—the absolute rigidity of the mental contents of human minds over a period of time sufficient to complete all actions contemplated at one time. The final price is a helpful concept for studying and understanding the formation of actual market prices.

HA. 244-250.

Final state of rest. An imagined or hypothetical state toward which every market action is a step but the attainment of which would mean that all market actions had ceased because man's attainable ends had all been attained and consequently there was no further cause for any more market actions. This state is never attained as man's ends are both unlimited and ever changing and every new end or shift in value scales sets off a new set of market actions tending toward a new and different final state of rest. Consequently, the final state of rest toward which all market actions are ever moving is constantly shifting before being reached. This imaginary construction is helpful as a guide to understanding current market movements at any specified time.

HA. 244-250.

Final wage rate.   See "Final price," *mutatis mutandis* (q.v.).

Fineness.   The proportion of the pure precious metal in gold or silver coins and bullion. American gold coins were 9/10th fine, while British gold coins were 11/12th fine.

Finite.   Having determinable limits; having a limited height or boundary; neither infinite nor infinitesimal; measurable.

Flexible standard.   Short for "Flexible gold exchange standard." A monetary system with a monetary unit for which the parity with gold is not fixed by law but is subject to instant change upon the order of some specified governmental agency. Under this standard, the movement of the unit's parity is almost always downward, since the primary purpose for adopting it is to hide or counteract the undesired ultimate effects of prior interventions, particularly those undertaken as the result of labor union pressures.

HA. 787-792; M. 429-430.

Flight into goods or real values.   The frantic rush to spend all monetary savings and other available cash, buying goods, whether needed or not, in order to avoid holding, even for a short time, any rapidly depreciating monetary units. This occurs at that point in the development of inflation when the public is convinced that prices will continue to rise endlessly and at an accelerated pace. The flight into goods or real values is also known as a "Crack-up boom" (q.v.) and marks the complete breakdown of a monetary system.

49

HA. 427, 436, 469-471, 550, 562; M. 227-230; also PLG. 165-166.

Foreign exchange. The currencies or media of exchange of other countries. In general usage, foreign exchange also includes negotiable instruments used for the international transfer of funds, such as checks, drafts and bills of exchange, which are payable in the currencies of other countries.

Foreign exchange rates are the exchange ratios between the currency of one country and the currencies of other countries. They are the prices or quotations for the currencies of other countries and are usually expressed in terms of the domestic currency.

HA. 452-458; M. 180-186.

Foreign exchange equalization account. A government fund set up under a "gold exchange standard" (q.v.) for handling the foreign exchange operations of the country's residents. The fund is usually established by a government grant of a certain quantity of gold and/or foreign exchange for its operations, which are normally carried on in secret in an attempt to stifle and hide from the public the inevitable effects of a domestic inflation and/or credit expansion. The foreign exchange equalization account of the United States is known as the Exchange Stabilization Fund.

HA. 461, 787; M. 429-430.

Free banking. A system in which banks would operate as private enterprises without any legal limitations, restrictions or privileges under such general laws, including those for bankruptcy, which are applicable to all types of free enterprise. Under such conditions banknotes would not be legal tender and the business of banks, including any issuance of banknotes, would be, like the business of other firms, solely dependent on their reputation and public acceptance.

HA. 443-448; M. 395-399.

French Revolution (1789). See "Revolution, French."

Frictional unemployment. See "Unemployment, frictional."

Führer, (German). Guide or leader, but not a pioneer. Title applied to Adolf Hitler (1889-1945), German Chancellor and

Führer (1933-1945). See "Nazi" and "National socialism."
S. 580-581.

Führertum, (German).   Leadership.
S. 580.

Fungible, n. and adj.   Capable of mutual substitution in use or satisfaction of a contract. A commodity or service whose individual units are so similar that one unit of the same grade or quality is considered interchangeable with any other unit of the same grade or quality. Examples—tin, grain, coal, sugar, money, etc.

Futures market.   A market for trading contracts wherein one party, usually a specialist, pledges for a certain sum of money to deliver to or buy from another party, the holder of the contract, a specified quantity of specified fungible commodities, securities or foreign exchange on a specified future date. Such contracts are primarily an extension of the division of labor principle whereby the speculative incidence of interim price changes are shifted from parties unfamiliar with the causes of such price changes to those with a special knowledge and understanding of expected price changes. Thus processors or manufacturers in need of future raw materials can know immediately the costs of such materials and foreign traders can likewise know immediately the domestic monetary equivalent of future payments for their exports or imports priced in foreign currencies.

G

Geist, (German).   Indwelling spirit of man; guiding mind or conscious intelligence. In the philosophy of Georg Hegel (1770-1831), only *Geist*—not matter—is reality. Hegel believed that *Geist* revealed to him the "truths" which he spoke and which became the official doctrines of the Prussian state and universities.

HA. 72-74; TH. 102-104.

Geology.   The science which deals with the history of the physical development of the structure, content and life of the earth as revealed by the application of the natural sciences to the physical formations found inside and on the surface of the earth.

German pattern of socialism.   See "Socialism of the German pattern."

Gestaltpsychologie, (German).   A school of psychology which holds that men grasp the meaning or reality of things according to the form, pattern, configuration or arrangement of the units or parts as they appear in the whole rather than in a breakdown or summation of the individual units, parts or sub-wholes of the wholes. Examples—a musical melody has greater significance to the hearer than the same tones played at random; three equal lines arranged as an equilateral triangle present an intellectual association of greater significance than the same lines otherwise arranged.

Thus, *Gestaltpsychologie,* unlike praxeology (q.v.), is not interested in studying the individual unit so much as it is concerned with the functional form or interrelationships of the units within the whole or universal.

Gettysburg Address (November 19, 1863). A short succinct speech delivered by President Abraham Lincoln (1809-1865) at the dedication of a National Cemetery on the American Civil War (1861-1865) battlefield at Gettysburg, Pennsylvania. It asks the living to dedicate themselves to the unfinished task "that this nation, under God, shall have a new birth of freedom; and that government of the people, by the people, for the people, shall not perish from the earth."

Glebe. Soil or farm land. Now used primarily in poetry. Once, the cultivable land belonging to, and used for the support of, a parish church.

Gleichschaltung, (German). Forced equalization, unification or synchronization.

Gold exchange standard. A national monetary system under which: (1) The domestic monetary unit is legally defined as the equivalent of a certain fixed weight of gold, called the parity rate; (2) Only money-substitutes (q.v.) are held by individuals and used in domestic business transactions, i.e., there are no domestic gold coins; (3) The national monetary authority maintains the value of all money-substitutes at the legally set parity rate by redeeming in gold such money-substitutes as a holder desires to use abroad at the legal parity rate or at rates between the gold export and import points (see "Gold points") of such parity; (4) The national monetary authority, as the only official domestic holder of gold and foreign exchange, exchanges all imports of gold and foreign exchange into domestic legal tender money substitutes at the legal parity rate or at rates between the gold export and import points of such rates. The gold exchange standard makes it possible for the national monetary authority to keep a part of its reserves not in gold but in foreign bank balances which are redeemable in gold. It was proposed by Ricardo (1772-1823) in 1816 as a monetary system which he believed would function the same as the gold standard by maintaining the value of domestic money-substitutes at the gold parity and would have the added advantage of economizing on the use of gold. In practice, the rigid gold exchange standard has permitted the political manipulation of the quantity of money. This in turn has led to inflation, credit expansion and the flexible gold exchange standard, or more simply the flexible standard (q.v.), under which the gold parity is subject to change, usually downward, whenever the government considers it advantageous, usually to prevent a further outflow of gold.

NOTE: In present day popular usage this term has been corrupted to mean a monetary system for which reserves are held in foreign currencies convertible into gold, as well as in gold itself. HA. 460-461, 786-793; M. 391-393, 407, 429-430, 451, 475; OG. 252.

Gold export point.   See "Gold points."

Gold import point.   See "Gold points."

Gold points.   The upper and lower limits beyond which the foreign exchange rates for a gold standard monetary unit cannot go without making it more profitable to ship gold than to buy or sell such foreign exchange. These limits are set by the costs of shipping gold into or out of the country and such costs include both interest and insurance. The limit beyond which it becomes more profitable to export gold is known as the gold export point, while the limit beyond which it becomes more profitable to import gold is known as the gold import point.

Gold standard.   A commodity money standard in which the commodity is gold. The gold standard is the sound monetary system, national or international, under which: (1) A monetary unit is defined as a certain fixed weight and fineness of gold; (2) Gold coins are used in business transactions and are part of the cash holdings of individuals; (3) Only standard gold coins have unlimited legal tender quality; (4) The national monetary authority is obliged to exchange without restriction gold against monetary units and monetary units against gold at the fixed rate or at such rate plus a sum not to exceed the costs of handling or minting; (5) The national monetary authority maintains the value of any and all subsidiary coins and paper money-substitutes at par with gold by remaining ready to redeem them on demand in gold at the parity rate and thus retire them from circulation; (6) There are no restrictions on the ownership of monetary gold or its movement into or out of the country.

The gold standard is an historical development of the market economy and as such a social institution for facilitating trade, both within and across national boundaries. The gold standard greatly limits the ability of banks and political authorities to manipulate short term market interest rates, the quantity of money and the purchasing power of the monetary unit. It thus acts as a deterrent of the trade cycle (q.v.). See also "Credit expansion" and "Monetary theory of the trade cycle."

HA. 428-429, 460-462, 471-476, 574, 782-783, 786-788; M. 20, 391, 394, 402, 407, 415-422, 429, 438, 448-450, 457; OG. 251-253; PF. 106; also PLG. xii-xiii, 153-154, 160-161, 168-169, 278-280.

Goods of higher orders. See "Goods, orders of."

Goods of the first, or lowest, order. See "Goods, orders of."

Goods, orders of. Economic goods (and services) are of different orders, depending on how far they are removed from their final production as a consumer's good (or service). Goods of the first or lowest order are goods ready for consumption by the final user (consumers' goods). Goods of the second order are producers' goods or factors of production (q.v.) which are one stage removed from being consumers' goods. Goods of the third order are two stages removed from consumers' goods and so on. Producers' goods and factors of production are referred to as "goods of the higher orders," or, when appropriate, "goods of the highest order."

HA. 93-94.

Gossen's law of the saturation of wants (first law of Gossen). The continuance, increase or repetition of the same kind of consumption yields a continuously decreasing satisfaction or pleasure up to a point of satiety. This law first propounded in 1854 by Hermann Heinrich Gossen (1810-1858), in a rare and little known German book, was rediscovered more than twenty years later by Robert Adamson (1852-1902), a Scottish Professor of Logic and Philosophy, and reported to the eminent English economist, William Stanley Jevons (1835-1882) who brought it to the attention of the economic profession.

PLG. 39-40.

Government. The social apparatus established for the monopolistic exercise of the compulsion and coercion which, because of man's imperfection, is necessary for the prevention of actions detrimental to the peaceful inter-human cooperation of a definite system of social organization. Because men are not faultless, government (the police power) is an indispensable and beneficial institution, as without it no lasting social cooperation or civilization could be developed or preserved. A durable system of government must rest on the might of an ideology acknowledged by the majority. The concept of a perfect system of government is both fallacious and self-contradictory, since this institution of men is based on the very imperfection of men. From the liberal (q.v.) viewpoint, the task of government consists solely and exclusively in guaranteeing the protection of life, health, liberty and private property against violent attacks. As far as the government confines the exercise of its violence to the suppression and prevention of antisocial actions, there prevails what reasonably and meaningfully can be called liberty.

AC. 90-91; B. 122-125; FC. 52; HA. 70-71, 149, 188-190, 197-198, 237-239, 280-287, 717-724; OG. 12, 46-51, 92, 119-120, 138, 247-248, 262-270, 284-286; S. 568; UF. 97-101; also PLG. 56-57, 108-109, 133-134, 159-160.

Greenbacks. Officially, United States Notes, first issued by the U.S. Treasury in 1862 as legal tender fiduciary paper money to help finance the Civil War (1861-1865). Their value in gold at one time (1864) was below 40 cents. In 1879, they became redeemable in gold. However, when the United States went off the gold standard in 1933, the greenbacks again became irredeemable. The highest amount outstanding was $450,000,000. There are still $347,000,000 outstanding, an almost insignificant part of the nation's legal tender today (1974).

Gresham's Law. Popularly stated: "Bad money drives out good money." More correctly stated: When a government recognizes more than one kind of money as legal tender, there is a tendency for the legally overvalued money to become the universally used medium of exchange, while the legally undervalued money disappears as a medium of exchange.

The earliest known recognition of this phenomenon is found in

The Frogs (405 B.C.) by the Athenian playwright, Aristophanes (448?-?380 B.C.). A translation reads: "The course our city runs is the same towards men and money. She has true and worthy sons. She has . . . coins untouched with alloys, gold or silver, each well minted, tested each and ringing clear. Yet, we never use them! Others always pass from hand to hand, sorry brass just struck last week and branded with a wretched brand. So with men we know for upright, blameless lives and noble names. These we spurn for men of brass. . . ." It was first discussed at length by a Frenchman, Nicholas Oresme (1320?-1382), Bishop of Lisieux after 1377. In his undated *Tractatus de Origine, Natura et Mutationibus Monetarium* he opposed the mutation of coins by Princes for their own gain. He declared such a debasement of coins unjust and intolerable because it demoralizes people, disturbs trade and leads to the disappearance of the precious metals from the country. The Polish astronomer, Copernicus (1473-1543), wrote in his *De Monetae Cudendae*: "That it is impossible for good-weighted coin and base and degraded coin to circulate together, That all the good coin is hoarded, melted down or exported; and the degraded coin alone remains in circulation."

This phenomenon was first called "Gresham's Law" in 1857, when the English economist, Henry D. McLeod (1821-1902) attributed it to Sir Thomas Gresham (1519-1579). A highly successful merchant, Sir Thomas, as a royal agent, advised England's Queen Elizabeth (1533-1603) on monetary reform. He pointed out that her father, Henry VIII (1491-1547), in "abasinge his quoyne" brought about a fall in the foreign exchange value of English coins and the departure of all fine gold from the realm. Actually, Gresham's Law is only a special case of the more general economic law that in a market economy no commodity is ever allocated to perform a function for which it is known that a cheaper commodity would serve as well.

EP. 86-88; HA. 435, 450, 760, 781-783, 786; M. 75, 442; also PLG. 152-154.

Gross (market) rate of interest. See "Interest, gross (market) rate of."

Guild socialism. An outgrowth of British (Fabian) socialism that emerged in the second decade of the twentieth century, gained considerable support after World War I and then faded into obscurity. It proposed the public ownership of all industries and the separate management of each industry by its workers, organized into a national guild or labor union. Its sponsors considered it an ideal social system which would eliminate "unearned income" (q.v.) and extend the principles of political democracy into the industrial realm. It was primarily an impractical reaction of some "democratic socialists" to the apparent dangers of an all powerful government, as noted in the Germany of the Hohenzollerns and later in the Soviet Union.

HA. 816-820; OG. 178; S. 258-262, 576, 584; UF. 130.

Guilds, or **Guild system** (originally "gilds"). Associations or corporations which originated in the Middle Ages. The most important were the Merchant Guilds and later the Craft Guilds which in fact were legal monopolies whose members were granted the exclusive right to practice a specified trade or craft within defined local areas. The Craft Guilds set wage rates, hours of work, apprenticeship terms and protected their privileges by holding membership below the demand for their services. The Guild system disintegrated with the rise of free market (liberal) ideas and industries with which they were unable to compete.

AC. 107

Guinea. The principal English gold coin during the period of legal bimetalism, from 1663 until the Act of 1816. Originally issued to pass as the legal equivalent of 20 shillings of silver, this ratio for many years overvalued silver so that the guinea passed at a premium. In 1717, a Royal decree forbade anyone to receive a guinea at any rate or value higher than 21 shillings. Since the Act of 1816, the guinea has become merely a nominal term for 21 shillings. Certain "quality" goods and services are still quoted in guineas rather than pounds sterling (q.v.).

HA. 471.

H

Habeas corpus, (Latin). Literally, an imperative, "have the body!" A legal document obtainable from a judge or court, on behalf of a person arrested and held without legally valid charge, which orders the jailer to release the prisoner immediately or to produce him before a judge or court and show a legal cause for his further detainment.

Harbinger. Originally, one who went ahead to prepare the way. Currently, a person, thing or event which precedes and foretells what is to follow; thus, an omen or forerunner.

Haute finance, (French). High finance. The big banks and bankers.

Hedonism. The theory that the final goal of all human action is pleasure, or rather happiness. For a careful discussion of *"Hedonism,"* see Henry Hazlitt's *The Foundations of Morality* (Princeton, N.J.: Van Nostrand, 1964; Los Angeles: Nash Publishing, 1972).
  EP. 151.

Hegelian dialectics. In the philosophy of Georg Hegel (1770-1831), the only reality is *Geist* (mind or spirit) and the only road to truth is by the dialectical process of logic. For him, logic, metaphysics and ontology were essentially identical. According to Hegel's peculiar thinking, dialectics proceeds from thesis to antithesis, i.e., the negation of thesis, and from antithesis to synthesis, i.e., the negation of the negation.
  AC. 36; TH. 102-106.

Hegemony. Leadership; predominant or controlling influence, especially that of someone in a position of authority, as a state government. As used in *Human Action,* it is a translation of the German term, *"Herrschaftlichkeit."* It refers to a position of authority, or belonging to a lord or master.

Heterogeneity. Diversity or variety in the individuals or elements of a mass or large group; absence of uniformity; opposed to homogeneity.

Heteronomous. Not self-determining; subordinate to something else; opposed to autonomous.

Heuristic. Helpful in the discovery of or revelation of truth; applied to arguments or methods which are persuasive rather than logically compelling, and which often lead one to search further for confirmation rather than to accept without question.

Historical School. A school of thought, originating in nineteenth century Germany, which held that a study of history was the sole source of knowledge about human actions and economic matters. This school contended that economists could develop new and improved social laws from the collection and study of statistics and historical data. An older group, before 1870, opposed the teachings of the Classical School (see "Classical economics"); while a later or younger group, after 1870, opposed the teachings of the Austrian School (q.v.) and advocated "social reform" by state action. The dominance of German universities by the Historical School resulted in the ridicule of "liberal" (q.v.) economics and the promotion of state socialism or national planning ideas. Thus the Historical School provided an ideological foundation for the German policies of the Nazi (q.v.) era. See also "*Methodenstreit.*"

   AS. 27-34; EP. x-xvii, 72; HA. 4, 62, 267-268, 605, 647, 761-762; S. 531.

Historicism. The theory of the Historical School (q.v.) that apart from the natural sciences, mathematics and logic, there is no knowledge but that provided by history. It appeals to the authority of tradition and the wisdom of the ages while opposing the ideas that inspired the American and French Revolutions. It now supplies support to socialism, interventionism and nationalism.
   HA. 4-6, 267-268; TH. 198-200.

Hoarding. An indefinite, and thus unscientific, term for cash holdings in excess of the quantity considered normal and adequate for the holder's needs.

60

HA. 381n, 402-405, 520-523; M. 35, 146-150; also PLG. 147-148, 157-165, 170, 280-281.

Holism, n. **holistic,** adj. The collectivist concept that one can learn all that one can learn by studying totals or the actions of whole units rather than the actions of individual men. Holism rests on the teleological or metaphysical faith that the actions of the whole somehow determine the actions of the parts rather than vice versa.

HA. 1, 145-153, as regards "money" 398-405.

Homo agens, (Latin). Man as an acting being.

Homogeneity, n. **homogeneous,** adj. The quality possessed by a grouping or aggregate whose parts or elements are all of the same kind, nature and character. Homogeneous units are units that are so essentially alike that they are capable of substitution one for another.

Homo oeconomicus, (Latin). Economic man (q.v.); a man driven exclusively by "economic" motives, i.e., solely by the intention of making the greatest possible material or monetary profit.

EP. 179-180; HA. 62-64, 239-243, 651-652.

Homo sapiens, (Latin). Zoological term for man as distinguished from other animals. Man is the reasonable animal. He uses his reason to guide his choice of actions by which he attempts to improve the external conditions of his life and well-being.

HA. 14, 25; OG. 121.

Homunculus. Small or little man, pygmy, dwarf, puny man, midget; often used in the sense of an artificial human being.

Hot money. Money in bank balances, demand loans on securities or short term investments which the owners may move without notice from one country to another and thus out of one currency into another in search of greater security or better terms. Hot money moves promptly on loss of confidence in a currency due to fear of depreciation, legal devaluation, or a legal limitation or prohibition on future transfers out of the country. When security is not a factor, hot money moves to those countries paying the highest interest rates, or otherwise offering better terms, such as shorter notice for withdrawal or guarantees against confiscation. NOTE: This is not the popular meaning that hot money is money

61

that is suspected or tainted because it was obtained by questionable or illegal means.

HA. 464-466.

Human action. Purposeful behavior; an attempt to substitute a more satisfactory state of affairs for a less satisfactory one; a conscious endeavor to remove as far as possible a felt uneasiness. Man acts to exchange what he considers will be a less desirable future condition for what he considers will be a more desirable future condition. Thinking and remaining motionless are actions in this sense. Human action is always rational (q.v.), presupposes causality and takes place over a period of time.

EP. 143, 149-150; HA. 11, 19, 22, 45, 97, 99, 223, 235, 479, 648, 653; UF. 34-36; also PLG. 1-20.

Humanité, (French). Mankind, society, humanity. NOTE: *Humanité* was used by the atheist, Auguste Comte (1798-1857), as the name for his religion, the religion of Humanity, which exalted a society altered according to Comte's ideas of perfection.

Huns. Barbaric Asiatic invaders who sacked and destroyed many cities of southern and central Europe during the fourth and fifth centuries A.D. Absolutely ruthless, they slaughtered and enslaved Europeans from the Caspian Sea to the Rhine and Loire Rivers, while living high on what they could plunder or exact in tribute. Their best known leader, Attila (406?-453) who exacted tribute from Rome, was turned back (451) by the combined armies of the Romans and Visigoths (Central European Germans of the era) at Châlons-sur-Marne (95 miles east of Paris) in one of the decisive battles of history.

Hydromechanics. The branch of physics concerned with the application of the laws of motion and equilibrium to liquids.

Hypostasis. Assignment of substance or real existence to concepts or mental constructs.

UF. 78-80.

Hypothesis. A seemingly reasonable explanation, supposition, or assumption proposed as a tentative answer to a problem in the absence of known or proven facts or causes. A hypothesis must not contain anything at variance with known facts or principles.

HA. 115.

I

Id. In psychoanalysis, the term applied to that part of the structure of the human mind from which subconscious urges and desires arise and out of which the Ego (q.v.) and the Super Ego (conscience and social norm controls) are said to spring.

HA. 12.

Ideal type. A rough generalization of a specific but loose concept helpful for the description and interpretation of history. An ideal type is a typification of a conceptual representation of complex reality by a grouping, each member of which has all or many of a number of specified distinctive qualities or characteristics. Because of its inexactness, an ideal type cannot be defined, but must be described by an enumeration of its basic features, all of which need not be present in any individual case. An ideal type may pertain to men, events, ideologies or human institutions. Examples are leader, bandit, king, dictator, town, state, nation, war, revolution, economy. Although the same terms may also be used in a precise legal or praxeological sense, their common or more general use lacks the precision and uniformity of praxeological terms and thus ideal types cannot form the basis for valid scientific laws or principles. They are, however, an indispensable tool for recording and understanding history.

EP. 75-79, 108-109; HA. 59-62, 251-252.

Ideology. (1) Any philosophical doctrine dealing principally with problems of society's political and economic organization. (2) In the Marxian usage of the term, a false doctrine that precisely on account of its falsity serves the interests of the class that developed it. Only in a classless society will men be able to develop truth free from ideological distortions. But the doctrines of Marx, Engels and other "proletarian" authors already anticipate, in the age of disintegrating "mature" capitalism, the perfect truth character of the science of the future. (3) The name of a French school of philosophy whose most eminent representatives were Pierre Jean George Cabanis (1757-1808) and Destutt de Tracy (1754-1836).

HA. 648; OG. 101-102, 119-120, 144-145; UF. 81-82, 130; also PLG. 68.

Ignoramus, (Latin). In law, we do not know. In a different American usage, an ignorant person.

Impalpable. Intangible; incapable of being felt; not readily obvious or intellectually perceptible.

Imperator, (Latin). Emperor. Originally, under the Republic of Rome (before 49 B.C.), it was the title given to an army commander after winning a great victory and was held only so long as he remained in command of troops. Later, the Roman Senate allowed such commanders to retain the title upon retirement. The first to use the title continuously was Julius Caesar (100-44 B.C.) who attained the rank with his first great victories in 58 B.C. When the Roman Empire was established in 27 B.C., the first ruler, Augustus (63 B.C.-14 A.D.) assumed the title Imperator and gave the word its present meaning, the supreme ruler of a state controlling a large territory, usually including a number of sub-states which had been conquered by the dominant state.

Imprescriptible. Eternally inalienable; permanently unalterable by law or authority; incapable of ever being disposed of or surrendered even if one wishes; absolute.

In abstracto, (Latin). In the abstract.

Increasing returns, law of. See "Returns, law of," of which it is a part.

Index numbers. Statistical averages of items selected as representative of all items of a class of economic data. Index numbers are usually designed to equal 100 for the base period and changes in their components are computed at regular intervals in an attempt to indicate general changes in a specific class of economic data.

The choice of the individual items and their weighting are of necessity arbitrary and unscientific. Index number comparisons must of necessity ignore all changes in the quality and relative importance of the individual items, including the introduction of new ones and the dropping of obsolete ones. Since most market participants are interested in specific items and not in averages, the significance of index numbers is greatly overrated. In times of inflation, index numbers for prices are at best crude and inaccurate indicators of changes in the exchange value or purchasing power of the monetary unit. See "Mathematical economics."

HA. 220-223, 351, 398-400, 442-443; M. 189-194, 201-203, 401-410.

Indirect exchange.   A two step exchange in which the first step is to exchange one's goods or services for a medium of exchange (q.v.), usually money (q.v.), and the second step is to exchange the medium of exchange so obtained for the goods or services desired. Indirect exchange contrasts with direct exchange (q.v.), i.e., barter or trucking, in which one trades his goods or services directly for the desired goods or services of another without the intermediary use of a medium of exchange, usually money. The need for indirect exchange increases as the division of labor increases and more goods and services become available for exchange.

HA. 202-204, 398-478; M. 29-34.

Induction, n. **inductive,** adj.   In logic, assuming the truth of a general (or universal) premise from the knowledge that individual or particular instances of the generality conform to the premise. Example: Assuming that all men speak English because all the men you know speak English.

Perfect induction is when the premise is based on the knowledge of all instances. In such cases, the induction is merely the statement of a known totality or generality.

Imperfect induction is when the premise is based on the knowledge of less than all the individual instances, i.e., on a sample. In the sciences of human action, imperfect induction can never provide scientific certainty. At best, it provides only a probability. However, imperfect induction is an epistemological basis of the natural sciences.

TH. 303; UF. 21-27, 44-45.

Industrial Revolution.   The rapid changes in the transition from medieval methods of production to those of the free enterprise system which took place from about 1760 to 1830, primarily in England. A term of Marxian origin loaded with emotional connotations in order to fit economic history into the theories of Fabianism (q.v.), Marxism (q.v.), Historicism (q.v.) and Institutionalism (q.v.).

B. 18; HA. 8, 617-623; OG. 101-102; PF. 136, 168.

Ineffable.   Incapable of being stated or described because of some elusive transcendental quality such as ideality, ethereality or spirituality.

Ineluctable.   Impossible to surmount or overcome; irresistible; inevitable.

Infant industries argument.   The argument that the domestic economy needs and can support certain new industries but that they cannot be started without the temporary assistance of a protective tariff until they grow large enough and efficient enough to compete with the already established industries of foreign nations. It is generally implied that the protective tariff will no longer be necessary after the industries have "matured" and that the nation will benefit in the long run from the early establishment of such industries.

HA. 509-510; also p.247 in Mises' article, "The Disintegration of the International Division of Labour," in *The World Crisis*, an anthology by the Professors of the Graduate Institute of International Studies at Geneva, Switzerland (London: Longmans, Green and Co., 1938).

Inflation.   In popular nonscientific usage, a large increase in the quantity of money in the broader sense (q.v.) which results in a drop in the purchasing power of the monetary unit, falsifies economic calculation and impairs the value of accounting as a means of appraising profits and losses. Inflation affects the various prices, wage rates and interest rates at different times and to different degrees. It thus disarranges consumption, investment, the course of production and the structure of business and industry while increasing the wealth and income of some and decreasing that of others. Inflation does not increase the available consumable wealth. It merely rearranges purchasing power by granting some to those who first receive some of the new quantities of money.

This popular definition, a large increase in the quantity of money, is satisfactory for history and politics but it lacks the precision of a scientific term since the distinction between a small increase and a large increase in quantity of money is indefinite and the differences in their effects are merely a matter of degree.

A more precise concept for use in theoretical analysis is any increase in the quantity of money in the broader sense which is not offset by a corresponding increase in the need for money in the broader sense, so that a fall in the objective exchange-value (purchasing power) of money must ensue.

NOTE: The currently popular fashion of defining inflation by one of its effects, higher prices, tends to conceal from the public the other effects of an increase in the quantity of money whenever the resulting rise in prices is offset by a corresponding drop in prices due to an increase in production. The use of this definition thus weakens the opposition to further increases in the quantity of money by political fiat or manipulation and permits a still greater distortion of the economic structure before the inevitable readjustment period, popularly known as a recession or depression (q.v.).

B. 84; HA. 414, 422-424, 427-428, 431-432, 548-571; M. 219-231, 239-241; OG. 215, 218-219, 251-254; PF. 50-51, 72-82, 88, 102, 127-128, 150-161; also PLG. 135-137, 146-147, 164-166, 176-295.

Inscrutable. Incapable of being analyzed and understood because the essential facts or factors are concealed.

Institutional. Relating to an institution in the sense of a humanly created and generally accepted social custom, usage, law, rule, principle or pattern of procedure or organization, etc., which pertains to, guides or regulates social conduct. Examples: Government, language, family, individual laws, private property, market society, money, etc. See also "Institutional economics" and "Institutionalism."

Institutional economics. An holistic school of thought (see "Holism"), of American origin, that maintains that the patterns of group behavior, rather than individual human actions, should occupy the central stage of "social studies." This school believes that man's activities are primarily fashioned by irresistible social pressures called institutions. Such institutions include custom, habit, tradition, environment and man-made law. Attributing the ills of mankind primarily to the institutions of *"laissez-faire* capitalism," they seek to change existing institutions by the pressures of public (i.e., politically controlled) education, political intervention and social controls (central planning) which they believe will eliminate the maladjustments and clashes of interest they consider inherent in a market economy based on private property and the self-interest of individuals. Institutional economics has been largely influenced by the writings of Thorstein Veblen (1857-1929), John R. Commons (1862-1945), Wesley C. Mitchell (1874-1948), the sociologist Charles H. Cooley (1864-1929) and the philosopher John Dewey (1859-1952). It is the American variety of the British and German Historical Schools of Economics. (See "Historical School.")

EP. xvii, 8; OG. 59; S. 531.

Institutionalism. An American outgrowth of Historicism (q.v.) which emphasizes control of human actions by patterns of group behavior and advocates political intervention as the best means of changing man's habits and improving mankind. The "institutional approach" is a collectivist approach opposed to the approach of individualism and the idea that economics is a science. Institutionalism is a broader and more general term than Institutional economics (q.v.).

EP. 8; HA. 647.

Institutional unemployment. See "Unemployment, institutional."

Interest, gross (market) rate of. The market interest rate which is the composite figure for originary interest (q.v.), plus or minus the entrepreneurial component (see "Interest rate, entrepreneurial component"), and plus or minus the price premium (q.v.). For Mises' detailed critical analysis of Böhm-Bawerk's interest theories referred to in *Human Action*, p.488n., see below, pp.150ff.

Interest, neutral rate of.   A uniform, originary rate of interest (see "Originary interest") in certain inconceivable imaginary constructions which assume neutral money (q.v.). With a neutral rate of interest, the interest rate on loans would always coincide with the ratio between the prices of present goods and the prices of future goods, under the assumption that all prices change uniformly.

HA. 538, 541-543.

Interest rate, entrepreneurial component.   The component of the gross or market interest rate which reflects the uncertainty element due to the entrepreneurial speculation present in every loan. The entrepreneurial component varies in each instance in accordance with the peculiar circumstances pertaining to the specific deal.

AC. 85-86.

International Monetary Fund.   An international monetary organization related to the United Nations (q.v.). The IMF was officially proposed during World War II at the 1944 Bretton Woods Conference (q.v.) and organized in 1946 with 38 member countries. As of June 1965, there were 102 member countries.

Each member country subscribes for a set quota, payable partly in gold (25% or less) and partly in their own currency. The United States quota is $4.1 billions, of which 25% was paid in gold and the balance in dollars. As of May 1965, paid up subscriptions, at official parity rates, totaled just over $15 billions. The Fund's resources are available, within limits, for member countries to borrow or purchase with their own currencies, at the legal parity, whenever any member country feels the need of additional assets to bolster public confidence in the gold parity of its currency, threatened by domestic policies of unbalanced budgets financed by inflation and/or credit expansion. (See "Bretton Woods Conference.")

PLG. 281, 285-286.

Interventionism. The doctrine or practice of the legally hampered market economy. (See "Market economy, the hampered.") The policy of resorting to governmental decrees and coercion to direct market activities in a manner different from the primary desires of consumers as expressed by the practices, prices, wage rates and interest rates of an unhampered market economy. (See "Market economy, the free or unhampered.") Interventionism is always an attempt to help some at the expense of others, as contrasted with the unhampered market economy in which participants improve their situations by improving the situations of others. Many interventionists, failing to understand economics, advocate specific interventions as a means of saving free enterprise from what they consider its excesses or weaknesses. [Interventionism was the policy advocated by Karl Marx (1818-1883) and Friedrich Engels (1820-1895) in the *Communist Manifesto* (1848) "as a means of entirely revolutionizing the mode of production." Later, both Marx and Engels repudiated interventionism as a *petit bourgeois* policy.]

For a complete analysis of all phases of interventionism, see *Human Action*, Part Six, pp.716-861.

AC. 58-62; B. 118-119; EP. 162-164, 218-222; OG. 58-66, 182-186, 192, 247-255, 267-271, 284-286; PF. 1-35; S. 531; also PLG. 52-54.

Introversive labor. Exertions which are ends in themselves in that they provide immediate inner satisfaction; as opposed to extroversive labor, exertions undertaken as a means to attain a desired end. Examples of introversive labor include religious activities, pleasurable, mental or physical exercises and exertions undertaken to divert one's mind from problems of the moment.

Ipso facto, (Latin). By the act or fact itself; by that very fact.

Iron Law of Wages. The doctrine according to which "the price of . . . labor is equal to its cost of production," that is "the means of subsistence that he [the worker] requires for his maintenance, and for the propagation of his race."*

---

* Quotations from the *Communist Manfesto*, Part I.

70

The Iron Law of Wages is an extension to the field of labor of the idea that the value of anything is found in its cost of production or reproduction. This alleged law holds that under capitalism, there is a natural law of wages toward which wage rates must constantly tend to return. This "natural" rate is that which provides a "subsistence level" for workers, wives and the raising to maturity of sufficient children to maintain the number of workers needed for the state of production. It is held that higher wages will result in raising more children to maturity, and lower wages in fewer, so that eventually the competition of more, or fewer, workers must drive wages back in line with the natural rate needed to sustain a sufficient number of workers. Founded on the writings of David Ricardo (1772-1823), the Iron Law of Wages was adopted by the German socialist, Ferdinand Lassalle (1825-1864), as well as his rival, Karl Marx (1818-1883). They used it as an argument to prove there was no hope for the workers under capitalism.

AC. 85; HA. 603-604.

Irrational. That which lies beyond the bounds of what can be comprehended, explained, justified or rejected by human reasoning and science. Antonym: rational (q.v.). NOTE: Irrational does *not* mean incorrect or impractical reasoning, but the total absence of any reasoning.

EP. 31-35, 135, 148; HA. 19-23, 89, 102-104, 173, 184-187, 884; OG. 112-113.

Irrationalism. The theory that human reason is unfit to interpret or elucidate the material forces that determine human behavior. Irrationalism attacks the very basis of praxeology and economics.

J

Jesuit padres . . . commonwealth (Paraguay). A theocratic mission which governed native Indians from 1605 to 1769. It started when Spain granted the Society of Jesus exclusive rights to rule an area in what is now Paraguay and which then was inhabited by 100,000 to 200,000 Guarani Indians. The previously savage Indians were transformed into docile and devoted Christian converts who obeyed orders to farm the land, build imposing churches and perform simple tasks for an ecclesiastical government that ran each community like a religious convent. The theocracy ended soon after Spain in 1767 suppressed the Jesuit order in all Spanish areas.

Jobber. A middleman who buys from importers, wholesalers or manufacturers for resale to other dealers, usually retailers. The term is mostly used in a deprecatory sense.

Judgment of relevance. The weight, appraisal or relative importance that one attaches or assigns to each of many factors that contribute to a multi-caused outcome of human actions. Judgments of relevance are not arbitrary preferences, like judgments of value (q.v.), but are sincere attempts to weigh the relative significance of all contributing factors. However, they are subjective and thus subject to variation between honest men or able experts.

   HA. 50, 55, 57-58, 88; UF. 102.

Judgment of Value. The outcome of mental acts of an individual, which cannot be observed but which express his wants, tastes, desires, feelings, choices or preferences which incite or impel him to act in a certain manner at a given time, situation and environment in an attempt to substitute conditions he prefers for those he considers less satisfactory. A judgment of value is personal and subjective and thus not open to proof or disproof. It can only be identified by an action from which it is inferred.

   EP. 35-37, 80; HA. 10, 21, 47-49, 56-57, 87, 94-97, 102-103, 119-122, 204, 242, 331-335, 354, 430, 652, 882-883; OG. 113; TH. 19-26; UF. 37-38.

K

Kadi, (Arabic). In Moslem countries, a judge or magistrate who exercised the judicial authority of the Sultan.

Kaleidoscopic. Characterized by an unending variety due to a constant shifting of the multitudinous elements which comprise the total.

Kathedersozialisten, (German). Academic socialists, or socialists of the chair; a term applied to the university professors of the Historical School (q.v.). These German professors were opponents of the Austrian School (q.v.) in the *Methodenstreit* (q.v.).

Keynesians. Advocates of the policies espoused by Lord John Maynard Keynes (1883-1946), particularly those contained in his *The General Theory of Unemployment, Interest and Money* (1936). In general, these policies are a restatement in new terminology of a number of previously refuted economic fallacies. Keynes denied Say's law of markets, believed general overproduction possible, disparaged savings and advocated both increased consumption and deficit spending as a remedy for recessions or depressions. His remedy for unemployment, created by the ability of politically protected labor unions to raise the wage rates of their members above those of the free market, was to lower the value of the monetary unit by credit expansion and inflation. He believed such an increase in the quantity of money would stimulate employment by increasing purchasing power which he called "effective demand." For a refutation of Keynesianism, see Henry Hazlitt's *The Failure of the "New Economics"* (Princeton, N.J.: Van Nostrand, 1959; New Rochelle, N.Y.: Arlington House, 1973), W. H. Hutt's *Keynesianism: Retrospect and Prospect* (Chicago: Regnery, 1963) and Henry Hazlitt, editor, *The Critics of Keynesian Economics* (Princeton, N.J.: Van Nostrand, 1960).
OG. 228; PF. 50-71, 98, 104; also PLG. 130-131, 261, 284.

King, Gregory, Law of. The law attributed to Gregory King (1648-1712) who estimated that a deficiency in the wheat harvest of:

> 10% would raise prices by 30%
> 20% would raise prices by 80%
> 30% would raise prices by 160%
> 40% would raise prices by 280%
> 50% would raise prices by 450%

This "law" or estimate was an advance over the still more crude formulation of the quantity theory of money which held that any drop in the supply would lead to a proportional rise in prices.

Ku Klux Klan. A secret American society organized at the close of the Civil War (1861-1865) for the purpose of re-establishing and maintaining local "white supremacy" in the South. During World War I, it was revived with members who were anti-Semitic and anti-Roman Catholic as well as anti-Negro. Its members dress in white sheets and hoods, particularly when engaged in threatening or criminal acts against those who have incurred their wrath.

L

Labarum. Roman military standard, later adopted by Emperors as Imperial Standard. Constantine the Great (288?-337), after his conversion to Christianity (312), wove the monogram of Christst (☧) into his standard, now known as the "labarum." Hence, a standard or symbol for which men live and die.

Labor Party (British). A British political party formed in 1900 at a meeting of trade unionists and socialists. Its political and economic ideas were largely supplied by the Fabian Society. (See "Fabianism.") The Party's first secretary, J. Ramsay MacDonald (1866-1937), became Prime Minister for ten months in 1924, when the 158 Liberal members of Parliament supported the 191 Labor members in opposition to a protectionist proposal of the 258 Conservative Party members. During this time Great Britain recognized the Union of Soviet Socialist Russia. Returned to power 1929-1931, with 288 members to Conservative 261 and Liberal 57, the Party's policies resulted in taking Great Britain off the gold standard. In power with a clear majority for the first time, 1945-1951, the Party socialized medicine, nationalized key industries and reduced the value of the British pound from $4.03 to $2.80. The Party's re-election in 1964 placed the pound in immediate jeopardy.

OG. 223-224; S. 539.

"l'acte per lequel nous ramenons à l'identique ce qui nous a, tout d'abord, paru n'être pas tel," (French). [Science is] "the process by which we are led back to the very thing which, at first, did not seem to us to be so."

HA. 38n.

"la durée pure, dont l'écoulement est continu, et où l'on passe, par gradations insensibles, d'un état à l'autre: Continuité réellement vécue," (French). Pure duration, in which the flow is continuous

and one passes by imperceptible degrees from one state to another: Continuity really lived (or experienced).

Laissez faire, (French).   Short for *laissez faire, laissez passer,* a French phrase meaning to let things alone, let them pass. First used by the eighteenth century Physiocrats (see "Physiocracy") as an injunction against government interference with trade. Now used freely as a synonym for free market economics, or what Mises prefers to call the unhampered market economy (see "Market economy, the free or unhampered").

AC. 83, 91; HA. 9, 619-620, 730-732, 748, 840; PF. 36-49, 58, 141, 177, 182; S. 323.

"la sympathie par laquelle on se transporte à l'intérieur d'un objet pour coïncider avec ce qu'il a d'unique et par conséquent d'inexprimable," (French).   "The sympathy with which one enters inside an object in order to identify thereby what it has that is unique and therefore inexpressible."

Latifundia, (Latin).   Large landed estates as owned by the old Roman aristocracy, the medieval lords and, at various historical periods, by the landed aristocracy in non-European lands. Most of them were originally obtained by conquest or as a reward for military assistance to a conqueror. They were worked by gangs of slaves, former prisoners of war or their descendants.

Latin Monetary Union.   A monetary union formed in 1865 by France, Belgium, Italy and Switzerland and later (1875) joined by Greece. While not members, Spain (1868), Rumania (1868), Bulgaria (1893), Serbia and Venezuela (1891) conformed with the policies of the Union.

After the gold discoveries in California and Australia in the mid-nineteenth century, the relative value of gold fell, resulting in the disappearance of silver coins. (See "Gresham's law.") The Union was formed to meet this situation. It attempted to preserve the French bimetallic ratio of 15½ ounces of silver to one of gold by providing for standard silver coins corresponding to the French five franc piece and gold coins for all higher denominations. A few years later, the relative value of silver began to fall and huge quantities of silver were presented for mintage while gold coins were disappearing. This led the Union to set quotas for the further coinage of the standard silver coins and later (1878) to suspend their coinage altogether. For all practical purposes, this placed the Union countries on the gold standard.

HA. 472; M. 75-76; also PLG. 149-151.

"la vie est une cause première qui nous échappe comme toutes les causes premières et dont la science expérimentale n'a pas à se préoccuper," (French). "Life is a first cause which eludes us, as all first causes do, and with which experimental science does not have to concern itself."

Law of participation. A concept of the French philosopher Lucien Lévy-Bruhl (1857-1939), wherein he holds that persons with a primitive mentality somehow believe there is a "participation" between persons and objects which are part of a collective representation. They see a sort of mystic communication and interrelation in collective representations that are wholly indifferent to contradictions apparent to nonprimitives. The parts of the collective are conceived of as both themselves and something other than themselves at the same time.

HA. 36-37; and see also Lucien Lévy-Bruhl's *How Natives Think,* trans. by L. A. Clare (New York, 1932), Chapter II.

League of Nations. An international association of the governments of member nations (1919-1946). Proposed during World War I by President Woodrow Wilson (1856-1924) of the United States, the League's covenant was incorporated in the Versailles Peace Treaty (1919). Its headquarters were at Geneva, Switzerland. Apart from its attempts to bring about order and lasting peace in international relations, it served as a collector of statistics, a preparer of reports and a meeting place for discussions by nationalist minded representatives of its member governments. It lacked the spirit of liberalism (see "Liberal") and thus failed to solve the major international problems of its era such as colonialism, political restrictions on international trade and investments and domestic interventionisms which led to international conflicts. Its failure to solve the Manchurian Crisis of 1931 led to the withdrawal of Japan (1933) and the League's gradual disintegration before World War II. It was formally dissolved in 1946, after the formation of the United Nations (q.v.). The United States never joined the League, although it did participate in many of its subsidiary activities, such as the International Labor Organization (1934), an organ for the promotion of "pro-labor" interventionism which has been continued under the United Nations.

FC. 147-151; HA. 687, 825; OG. 4-7, 280-281.

Lebensraum, (German). Literally, space for living or existence. The Nazi (q.v.) *Lebensraum* policy was a policy of territorial expansion aimed at acquiring "a fairer distribution" of the world's raw materials so as to provide Germans with *Nährungsfreiheit* (freedom from importing food) and a standard of living equal to the world's highest.

HA. 324; OG. 1, 74-78, 217, 234, 236, 261; S. 554, 579.

Legal tender. A legal medium of payment. Money (q.v.) or media of exchange (q.v.) which the law requires a creditor to accept at face value when offered (tendered) in payment of any outstanding monetary debt or obligation. In practice, a law bestowing legal tender quality affects only monetary obligations already contracted.

HA. 450, 780, 783-785; M. 69-71.

Leiturgia, (old Latin, from the Greek). Liturgies. Compulsory public services which the wealthy must perform or subsidize for the state; a sort of special tax levied on the rich in the ancient Greek city states, such as Athens, and later in both Egypt and the Roman Empire. Originally, the well-to-do were required to aid without remuneration in the execution of important public works, such as collecting taxes, serving as public officials, providing food for the poor in times of famine, furnishing food and quarters for the army, supplying animals and drivers or outfitting ships for the transport of men and goods the state wanted moved, etc. Later, these liturgies became a means for those in power to despoil the wealth of large property owners and others not in political favor, with the result that they hastened economic decay.

"Le moulin à bras vous donnera la société avec le souzerain; le moulin à vapeur, la société avec le capitaliste industriel." Marx, *Misère de la philosophie,* p. 100, (French). "The handmill gives you society with the feudal lord; the steam-mill, society with the

industrial capitalist." Marx, *The Poverty of Philosophy* (English translation of the German), p. 105.

HA. 79n.

Lend-lease. A United States law (March 17, 1941) providing financial assistance for governments fighting Nazi Germany and, after December 7, 1941, Japan. When World War II started in Europe (1939), American neutrality laws stipulated that all sales of war supplies must be paid for in cash and shipped in foreign vessels. French and British orders paid for by gold shipments soon ended the mass American unemployment of the 1930s. By July 1940, France had fallen and Great Britain had informed the American government secretly that "it will be utterly impossible for them to continue" to pay cash indefinitely. After the November election the British situation was made public and the President requested Congress to pass the Act which gave him the power to sell, lend, lease or give away such war supplies as he considered necessary for the aid of countries "whose defense is vital to the United States." The total aid provided under this law (1941-1948) exceeded $50 billion.

S. 556; also PLG. 245-246.

Level of prices. See "Price level."

Liberal. (1) Used by Mises "in the sense attached to it everywhere in the nineteenth century and still today in the countries of continental Europe. This usage is imperative because there is simply no other term available to signify the great political and intellectual movement that substituted free enterprise and the market economy for the precapitalistic methods of production; constitutional representative government for the absolutism of kings or oligarchies; and freedom of all individuals for slavery, serfdom, and other forms of bondage." (HA. v). NOTE: In the Third Edition of *Human Action* the last "for" appeared in error as "from."

(2) "In the [early nineteenth century] constitutional conflict in Spain in which champions of parliamentary government were fighting against the absolutist aspirations of the Bourbon Ferdinand VII, the supporters of a constitutional regime were called Liberals and those of the King Serviles. Very soon the name 'Liberalism' was adopted all over Europe." (UF. 92)

Mises considers true liberalism to be the practical philosophy of scientific praxeology (q.v.) and economics (q.v.). See especially FC., which appeared originally (1927) as *Liberalismus* (Liberalism). The English-Language Edition carries the subtitle, *"An Exposition of the Ideas of Classical Liberalism."* Its appendix discusses the term "Liberalism" and the "Literature of Liberalism."

AC. 92-94; HA. 149-150, 153-157, 174-175, 183, 285, 324, 689-690, 864-866; OG. 2, 18-32, 48-51, 75, 80-81, 89-96, 136, 281-284; S. 48-49, 57, 70, 71, 74, 76-78, 83, 310, 319-320, 323-324, 326, 403, 423, 462-463, 501-504.

Litigious. Inclined toward lawsuits or judicial disputes. Also, subject to legal argument or dependent upon a judicial decision.

Logical positivists. Adherents of the modern British and American variety of positivism (q.v.). This school has been influenced largely by the teachings of the so-called Vienna Circle founded in 1924 by Moritz Schlick (1882-1936). The chief exponents of this school have been Otto Neurath (1882-1945) and Rudolf Carnap (1891-1970). The significance of the logical positivists for the study of Mises' *Human Action* lies in the fact that their fundamental thesis rejects all non-experimental methods of research and thus denies the existence of any *a priori* knowledge.

TH. 240-250; UF. 5, 39, 53, 70, 123.

"l'on ne peut le pratiquer sans s'être demandé si les deux objets échangés sont bien de même valeur, c'est-à-dire échangeables contre un même troisième," (French). "One cannot practice it [exchange] without having asked himself whether the two objects exchanged are goods of the same value, that is to say [goods] exchangeable for a third [good] with the very same value."

Loss. The effect of unsuccessful human actions which result in distress (psychic loss, see "Psychic profit and loss") and/or a decrease in net assets (entrepreneurial loss, see "Entrepreneurial profit and loss"). Losses are primarily ascribed or assigned to those who would have received the profits if the actions had been successful.

Lucubration. Belabored study; serious treatise; product of long and serious thought.

M

Malinvestment. An investment in wrong lines which leads to capital losses. Malinvestment results from the inability of investors to foresee correctly, at the time of investment, either (1) the future pattern of consumer demand, or (2) the future availability of more efficient means for satisfying a correctly foreseen consumer demand. Example of (1): An investment of available savings in a manner that cannot produce as much consumer satisfaction as the same funds could produce if invested differently. Example of (2): An investment which, before the end of its expected useful life, becomes obsolete due to the unforeseen development of more efficient means for satisfying the same consumer demand. Malinvestment is always the result of the inability of human beings to foresee future conditions correctly. However, such human errors and the resulting malinvestments are most frequently compounded by the illusions created by undetected inflation (q.v.) or credit expansion (q.v.). From the viewpoint of attaining maximum potential consumer satisfaction, every political intervention, other than that needed for the preservation of the market society, must lead to malinvestment.

HA. 394, 550-565, 576, 580-586; M. 314-318, 357-366; also PLG. 187, 198-199, 205, 249-251.

Malthusian law of population. A special case of the law of returns first propounded and revised by Thos. R. Malthus (1766-1834) in six editions (1798-1826) of his *An Essay on the Principle of Population.* This law holds that, other things being equal, population tends to increase by geometrical progression (1, 2, 4, 8, etc.), while the means of subsistence tend to increase by arithmetical progression (1, 2, 3, 4, 5, etc.) so that unless "moral restraint" or "preventive checks" are exerted, the excess increase in population will inevitably be removed by such "positive checks" as war, vice, poverty, disease, starvation and widespread plagues and famines.

HA. 129-130, 667-672.

Mammonist. Prompted by the desire for material wealth or financial gain.

Manchester School, Manchesterism. A group of active British advocates of *laissez faire*, free trade, limited government principles who maintained that a wider practice of such principles would reduce international frictions and lead to world peace. The name derives from Manchester, England, where the leading merchants and manufacturers reconstituted the Chamber of Commerce in 1820 in order to protest existing protectionist policies. In this milieu, the Anti-Corn Law League (see "Corn Laws") held its first meeting in Manchester in 1838. The Manchester School was influential in shaping many British political policies during the next fifty years. Before the turn of the century, popular support gradually switched to the interventions advocated by the Conservative Party and later those promoted by the Fabian Socialists (see "Fabianism"). The best known and most influential leaders of the Manchester School were Richard Cobden (1804-1865) and John Bright (1811-1889).

FC. 199; HA. 238, 823, 828, 831; PF. 58; S. 541.

Mandarins, (from the Portuguese). Chinese public officials who were entitled to wear a button and maintain a superiority over and toward the general public.

Mandatary. An agent or representative chosen to follow the orders or commands of those who selected him; usually applied to legislators elected to carry out the instructions (mandates) of the voters.

OG. 137.

Mandats territoriaux, (French). Paper notes issued as currency (q.v.) by the French Revolutionary Government in 1796. They were land-warrants supposedly redeemable in the lands confiscated from royalty, the clergy and the church after the outbreak of the Revolution in 1789. In February 1796, 800,000,000 francs of mandats were issued as legal tender to replace the 24,000,000,000 francs of assignats then outstanding. In all about 2,500,000,000 francs of mandats were issued. They were heavily counterfeited and their value depreciated rapidly within six months. In February 1797, they lost their legal tender quality and by May were worth virtually nothing. See "Revolution, French."

Mandrake. An herb of the potato family found in the Mediterranean area. Once the object of many superstitions, its magical powers are now in disrepute. Women once ate its fruit to promote pregnancy and its roots were much esteemed as a love philter, a promoter of personal prosperity and aid to an oracle's powers of prophecy.

Manorial system or **organization.** See "Feudalism."

Manumission, n. **manumit,** v. Emancipation; the act of setting slaves free; the formal release from slavery.

Marginal producer. The producer who would be eliminated from competition by a drop in the market price or a rise in his production costs because his production costs are the nearest (at the margin) to the current market price. A marginal producer operates at little or no profit so that any unfavorable change in price or costs would make his further operation unprofitable.
 OG. 246-249.

Marginal productivity [of factors of production (q.v.)]. The market value imputed or attributed to the use of one more, or one less, unit, i.e., the marginal unit, of labor or a material factor of production. In a free market economy (see "Market economy, the free and unhampered"), wage rates and prices paid for the material factors of production constantly tend to coincide with the productivity of the marginal unit used or employed because entrepreneurs seek to (1) expand their production whenever more units are available for less than the value their use can add to production, and (2) reduce their production whenever a marginal unit costs more than consumers are expected to pay for the value added to production by that unit.
 AC. 86-89.

Marginal theory of value. The theory that the value assigned to any good is the importance attached to its use in removing some felt uneasiness and that the value of any unit of a supply of identical goods is the value assigned to the least important (or marginal) use for which the contemplated number of available units are expected to be used. This is so because a judgment of value always refers solely to the supply with which a concrete choice is concerned, for it is only the use of this specific (marginal) supply that one must decide to acquire or forego. Since each additional unit of an identical good will be allocated to a lesser valued use than was previously possible, the value attached to each additional (marginal) unit will be lower than that assigned to previously held units. Conversely, with each decrease in the number of units held, there will be an increase in the value of the least important (marginal) use to which the decreased available supply can be applied. The marginal theory of value is the subjective theory of value which is basic to all the theories of the Austrian School of Economics (q.v.). See also "Subjective-value theory."

HA. 119-127, 204-205, 636-637; also PLG. Ch. II (27-54), 70-91, 164-165.

Marginal utility. The least important use to which a unit of a contemplated supply of identical goods can be put. It is this least important or marginal use which is weighed or considered when one chooses to increase or decrease his supply by one unit, since this is the use (or value) which is to be obtained or renounced.

HA. 119-127, 636-637; also PLG. Ch. II (27-54), 70-91, 158-159, 164-165.

Margin monopoly. A monopoly for which there is an upper limit (marginal point) beyond which the monopolist cannot raise his monopoly price (q.v.) without inviting competition. A marginal monopoly is possible only when the ability to charge monopoly prices is dependent upon an exclusive advantage which is limited for either natural or institutional reasons, as in such cases where the monopolist enjoys greater fertility, richer ores, greater productivity, location or transportation advantages, tariff protection, governmental subsidies or price controls, etc.

Mark, (German).   The German monetary unit from 1873 until its breakdown in 1923. Convertible into gold ($0.2382) up to July 31, 1914 (World War I), the *Mark* remained the only legal tender in Germany until October 11, 1924.

On July 31, 1914, Germany had 4 billion gold *Marks,* of which 2.75 billions were in circulation and the balance were held as reserves against Reichsbank deposit liabilities and about 2 billion outstanding paper *Marks,* all redeemable in gold. By the end of 1918 the gold reserve was 2.5 billion *Marks* and the unredeemable notes outstanding 32.65 billions. By November 15, 1923, the irredeemable Reichsbank notes outstanding had reached 92,844,- 721,000 billion *Marks.* By the end of December 1923, they reached 496,507,425,000 billion *Marks* against which official gold reserves were the equivalent of only $111,200,000.

A decree of October 15, 1923 established the Rentenbank and provided for a transitional *Rentenmark* to be issued after November 15, 1923 with a value proclaimed to be the equivalent of 1,000 billion paper *Marks.* The volume of Reichsbank notes continued to increase for several months after the introduction of the *Rentenmark,* reaching 1,520,511,000,000 billion *Marks* by the end of September 1924. As a result of the Dawes Plan loan of 800,000,000 gold *Marks,* the Reichstag passed the Act of August 30, 1924 which provided for a gold *Reichsmark (RM)* on October 11, 1924, with one *RM* equal to 1,000 billion paper *Marks.*

Market economy, the free or unhampered.   A pure or unhampered (i.e., free) market economy is an imaginary construction which assumes: (1) The private ownership (control) of the means of production; (2) The division of labor and the consequent voluntary market exchanges of goods and services; (3) No institutional interferences with the operation of the market processes which generate prices, wage rates and interest rates which reflect the actual conditions of supply and demand for all goods and services; (4) A government, the social apparatus of coercion and compulsion, which is intent on preserving market processes while protecting peaceful market participants from the encroachments of those who would resort to the threat or use of force or fraud.

B. 36-39; HA. 237-239; OG. 48-51, 61, 64, 182, 246-247, 284-286.

Market economy, the hampered. A market economy in which the government interferes with the marketing processes by orders and prohibitions which divert the production of wealth from those channels which reflect the first choices of market participants. In short, the government does not limit its activities to the preservation of the private ownership (control) of the means of production and the protection of market participants from the encroachments of those who resort to the threat or use of force or fraud. See "Interventionism."

HA. 716-861; OG. 247-249, 284-286.

Market process. The voluntary and peaceful complex interaction of men deliberately striving toward the best possible removal of human dissatisfaction. The leadership in the process is assumed by promoters, speculators and entrepreneurs competing for the profits awarded to those who prove themselves superior in providing the most valued means for satisfying human desires. Every step in the market process depends on human decisions so that there is nothing automatic or mechanical in the process. By an inseparably interrelated series of human actions the market process determines the price structure of the market, the allocation of the factors of production and the share of each participating individual in the combined result.

HA. 333-338; also PLG. 65-91.

Marxism. The socialist theories of Karl Marx (1818-1883) and his collaborator and financial backer, Friedrich Engels (1820-1895). See *Das Kapital.* For an elaboration and comparison with other brands of socialism, see Mises' *Socialism.*

AC. 67; B. 57-58, 87, 98-100, 108; HA. 5, 9, 74-79, 235, 265, 267, 582, 616, 674-675, 693-695, 865-866, 877; OG. 59, 70, 112, 150-155; PF. 95-101, 159; TH. 102-158; also PLG. 31-39, 49, 109, 116-117, 175, 288.

Materialism. This term is used in two different senses: (1) The mentality of those who prefer material wealth, bodily comforts and sensuous pleasures over the "higher" intellectual and "nobler" spiritual aspirations of men; (2) The doctrine that all changes are brought about by material entities, processes and events, and that all human ideas, choices and value judgments can be reduced to material causes which one day will be explained by the natural sciences.

HA. 17, 154, 193, 216; TH. 75, 94, 152; UF. 28-33.

Material productive force.   A Marxian concept, or perhaps catchword, that Marx never adequately defined. Marx regarded the stage or conditions of production not only as a fact entirely independent from human thought but also as the determinant of human thought and social conduct. See *"Le moulin . . . "* (above).

AC. 36-37; HA. 79-80, 141-142; S. 302-303, 352-354; TH. 106-112; UF. 30-33.

Mathematical economics, or **Mathematical methods of economics.** The attempts to express or develop economic truths by means of mathematical formulas, equations or expressions which reflect a mechanical constancy in human actions and reactions that is contrary to the known nature of man. Often such attempts merely depict imaginary states of equilibrium, or nonaction, rather than the unmeasurable processes whereby individuals select, pursue and alter their actions, goals and value judgments, each in his own way as he is differently motivated at different moments. The processes of the market (see "Market process"), which are directed by the processes of the human mind, are grading, preferring, choosing, exchanging and setting aside, amidst everchanging conditions of human understanding and physical availabilities. Since these processes are mental, qualitative and unmeasurable rather than automatic, mechanical or measurable, they are not subject to mathematical presentations which are always quantitatively precise, but unable to portray qualitative differences.

While mathematical presentations may possibly help in depicting certain market tendencies, as in the use of supply and demand curves, it must be realized that all mathematical representations which do not stand for historical data are merely imaginary assumptions about which there can be no certainty as to whether or not they represent present or future reality. Mathematical methods are based on unscientific assumptions, give false impressions of precise reality and too often divert attention from the logical solution of economic problems. Each such problem can only be solved by the selection of the successive steps that must be taken over a period of time in order to attain a realizable desired goal in a world in which the uncertainties of the future cannot be known or presented mathematically in advance. See "Econometrics," a branch of mathematical economics, and "Quantitative economics."

> EP. 116-118, 165; HA. 250, 256, 333, 350-357, 377-379, 399, 701-703, 710-715; PF. 148-149; UF. 4; also PLG. 42, 46-47, 61.

Mediate. Indirect; means to; cause of; intermediate step to; intervention leading to.

Mediatized families. Families of the princes and counts of the Holy Roman Empire who since the thirteenth century had step-by-step acquired a quasi-sovereign position in their territories and then were deprived of this quasi-sovereign position early in the nineteenth century. However, they retained their titles and certain minor privileges until the end of World War I. See *"Standesherr."*

Medieval scholasticism. The intellectual speculations and doctrines of the leading philosophers of the Middle Ages, roughly 800-1400 A.D. Their main discussions revolved around such controversies as the reality of universals (nominalism [q.v.] vs. realism), man's free will (determinism vs. indeterminism) and the compatibility of logic with Christian theology (reason vs. revelation). The most noted medieval scholastic, or schoolman, was St. Thomas Aquinas (1225-1274), a moderate realist.

Medium (media, pl.) of exchange. Any good, such as money (q.v.), which people seek for use in exchange rather than for consumption or use in production. A highly marketable good for which one first exchanges his less marketable wares or services so as to be able to offer a more acceptable good to the sellers of goods and services one seeks to buy. Any good which, because of popular acceptance, serves to facilitate indirect exchange (q.v.).

> HA. 208-209, 398, 401-402, 462-466, 780; M. 29-34; also PLG. 141-144, 153-154, 163.

Meliorism. The belief that both the morals and the reasoning powers of the masses are essentially sound so that with the innovation of democratic government their good judgment will inevitably make the world an ever better place for mankind in that all future changes will be progressive steps toward social perfection. HA. 191-193, 693-695; TH. 171-173.

Menshevik, (Russian). Literally "a member of the minority." A member of the Russian Social Democratic party who, for the realization of socialism, advocated less violent and more democratic methods than those advocated by the Bolsheviks (q.v.) from whom they split in 1903. After the November 1917 Russian Revolution, the one-party Communist dictatorship established by the Bolsheviks suppressed all opposition movements, including that of the Mensheviks.
S. 547.

Mercantilism. The theories of some sixteenth and seventeenth century writers based on the belief that the gain of one man or one nation must represent the loss of another and that the precious metals were always the most desirable form of wealth. In an attempt to increase a nation's wealth, they advocated the national regulation of foreign trade in a manner they thought would increase merchandise exports and hamper merchandise imports, thus creating an inflow of the precious metals. This is still called a "favorable balance of trade." The nineteenth and twentieth century advocates of such policies are called neo-mercantilists. See "Balance of payments."
HA. 53, 451-452, 456, 664; TH. 30, 297.

Mercenaries. Professional soldiers and soldiers of fortune who serve the country offering them the highest pay. Also, soldiers who serve a country other than their own for money.

Metalogical. Beyond the scope or province of logic.

Metamorphosis. Transformation, with the implication that the change is so abrupt and extreme that it is made as if by magic.

Metaphysics, (from the Greek). Beyond or after physics. The area of human thoughts and convictions that lie beyond the realm of scientific human knowledge and experience and therefore in the realm of beliefs, creeds, intuition, theology or supernatural revelation. Such thoughts or convictions are incapable of scientific proof and frequently, although not always, of disproof.
EP. 49; HA. 25-26, 32, 146-153.

Methodenstreit, (German). A dispute, argument or controversy over methods; specifically, the controversy over the method and epistemological character of economics carried on in the late 80's and early 90's of the nineteenth century between the supporters of the Austrian School of Economics (q.v.), led by Carl Menger (1840-1921), and the proponents of the (German) Historical School (q.v.), led by Gustav von Schmoller (1838-1917). The Historical School contended that economists could develop new and better social laws from the collection and study of statistics and historical materials. Their thought dominated German universities in the last half of the nineteenth century. This led to the ridicule of "liberal" (q.v.) economics in the universities. It thus assisted the growth of state or socialist planning which in turn paved the way for Nazi (q.v.) ideas.

AS. 27-34; EP. 72, 107, 123-124, 139-140.

Middle Ages. The period roughly from the fifth to the fifteenth centuries A.D., that is, from the fall of Rome in 476 A.D. to the fall of the Byzantine Empire in 1453, the invention of the printing press by Johann Gutenberg (1400?-?1468) and the discovery of America in 1492 by Christopher Columbus (1451-1506). During most of this period the leaders of the Roman Church considered the taking of interest (usury) unjust. This period, particularly the earlier part of it, is also known as the Dark Ages because of its intellectual and economic stagnation.

Mir, (Russian). A rural peasant village or community. In Russia before the modern reforms, the serfs of the Crown and those of some nobles lived in *Mirs,* where they elected their village assembly or council responsible for the collection of rent and taxes. When serfdom was ended in 1861, the government reimbursed the land-owning nobles and assigned title to some of the land to the *Mirs* which were required to make long term payments to the government. The land was thus owned in common by the peasants of the *Mir,* each of whom was assigned a plot of land to farm. The village assembly elected an elder who administered tax collections and from time to time allocated the commonly owned land among those entitled to farm it. The system failed to sustain the growing population and was abolished in 1906.

Modern theory of value. In Mises' terminology, the value theory generally known as the "Marginal theory of value" (q.v.) or "Subjective theory of value" (q.v.).

Molar. In mechanics: Pertaining to a mass or body as a whole, as opposed to molecular; acting as an aggregate unit and not as a group of separate parts.

Moloch. In the Old Testament of the Bible, the supreme deity of Semitic heathenism whom the men of Judah once appeased by the sacrifice of their dearest possession, their own children. Hence, any evil and vicious doctrine which requires the sacrifice of human lives.

Monetary theory of the trade cycle. The Mises explanation of the trade cycle (q.v.) showing how credit expansion (q.v.) creates a "boom" which makes an ensuing readjustment period inevitable. This readjustment period is popularly known as a "depression" (q.v.). See *Human Action*, Chapter XX, pp. 538-586, particularly Sections 8 and 9, pp. 571-586. For a more detailed analysis, see Mises' *The Theory of Money and Credit*, Murray N. Rothbard's *America's Great Depression* (Princeton, N.J.: Van Nostrand, 1963; Los Angeles: Nash Publishing, 1972) and PLG. 175-293.

Money. The most commonly used medium or media of exchange (q.v.) in a market society. A community's most marketable economic good, which people seek primarily for the purpose of later exchanging units of it for the goods or services they prefer. The circulating media most readily accepted in payment for goods, services and outstanding debts. Money is an indispensable factor in the development of the division of labor and the resulting indirect exchanges on which modern civilization is based. For the different types of money, see "Money in the broader sense," "Money in the narrower sense" and "Money-substitutes."
  HA. Ch. XVII (pp. 398-478); M. 29-34, 50-67, 79-90; also PLG. Ch. V (pp. 141-174), 183-184.

Money-certificate. In essence, a negotiable warehouse receipt for deposited money. A claim to a specific quantity of commodity money (q.v.) for which the issuer or his agents maintain a 100%

91

reserve of commodity money which is payable on demand and surrender of the certificate. Money-certificates are money-substitutes (q.v.) and money in the broader sense (q.v.). However, the certificates and the reserves held against them are considered one and the same quantity of money and should not be counted twice in arriving at the total quantity of money.

HA. 432-433, 435; M. 133-134, 483.

Money in the broader sense. Everything commonly used as money or readily convertible to money at face value. Money in the narrower sense and all money-substitutes (q.v.), including token money and fiduciary media. NOTE: While the term "money in the broader sense" includes both money in the narrower sense and all forms of money-substitutes, the quantity of money in the broader sense excludes any duplication of claims to money in the narrower sense and such money in the narrower sense that is held as a reserve against such claims. Money in the broader sense is the basic economic definition of money, as distinguished from legal definitions. It is the sense in which the term "money" is used in discussions of the problems of catallactics (q.v.) and the money relation (q.v.).

HA. 428-444, 448-450; M. 50-67, 482-483.

Money in the narrower sense. Money proper as distinguished from commonly used money-substitutes (q.v.). It includes the following: commodity money (gold coin), credit money (claims to money not readily redeemable) and fiat money (money solely by reason of law) when commonly used as media of exchange. It does *not* include the following: token money (minor coins), money-certificates (redeemable claims to money) and such fiduciary media (q.v.) as bank notes and deposits against which the monetary reserves are less than one hundred percent. Money in the narrower sense is more a legal than an economic category.

HA. 428-434; M. 50-62, 482-483.

Money proper. See "Money in the narrower sense."

Money relation. The relation between the demand for money (cash holdings in the broader sense) and the quantity of money (in the broader sense). Every change in either the demand for money or the quantity of money alters this relation and sets in motion forces which step by step change individual prices and the complex of production, while making some individuals richer and some poorer. Each such change also affects market interest rates. When the force has spent itself and is not able to affect any further changes, the final result of every change in the money relation is an altered interrelationship of individual prices (price structure).

HA. 411-432, 458-462, 548-550; M. 123-165.

Money-substitutes. Claims to money convertible at face value on demand. Anything generally known to be freely and readily exchangeable into money proper, i.e., money in the narrower sense, whether or not a legal requirement to do so exists. Money-substitutes include token money (minor coins), money-certificates (issuer maintains 100% reserves in money proper) and fiduciary media (issuer maintains less than 100% reserves in money proper). Fiduciary media in turn include both banknotes and bank deposits subject to check or immediate withdrawal. Money-substitutes serve all the purposes of money proper. They are part of money in the broader sense and a factor in the consideration of all catallactic problems as well as those affecting the money relation (q.v.).

HA. 427, 432-444, 448-450, 464, 472; M. 50-59, 482-483.

Mongol, Mongolian. Originally a native of Mongolia, Asia. In the twelfth and thirteenth centuries the Mongols conquered most of Asia and Eastern Europe. (See "Tartars.") Mongols are one of the five species of mankind. (See "Caucasian.")

S. 555.

Monism. The doctrine that both mind and matter can be reduced to one substance or ultimate reality.

HA. 17, 25, 716; UF. 115-124.

Monometallism. A monetary system which uses only one metal as the standard money and in which the monetary unit is defined as a specified weight and fineness of that metal. An example is the gold standard (q.v.).

Monopoly, monopolist. These terms have two distinctly different meanings: (1) A state of affairs in which an individual or group of individuals has the exclusive control of one of the vital conditions of human survival. In this situation, the monopolist is the master and the rest are slaves. It is the pattern of the socialist state (see "Socialism") and has no reference to a market economy. (2) A state of affairs in which an individual or a group of individuals has the exclusive control of the supply of a definite commodity or factor of production. In this sense, every market participant is a monopolist if the commodity or service he offers cannot be exactly duplicated by a competitor. Such a monopoly is of no importance unless market conditions permit the monopolist to charge monopoly prices (q.v.), which they rarely do without government interventionism (q.v.).

   HA. 277-278, 358-379, 383-387, 680-681; OG. 70-78, 248, 284; also PLG. 94-95, 98-99, 173.

Monopoly gain.   The income or increase in net worth earned by a monopolist in a position to charge monopoly prices.

   HA. 360-361, 363-365, 368-369, 371-376, 378, 383.

Monopoly price.   The price which emerges when a monopolist (q.v.) gains more from selling a smaller quantity of his monopolized good than he would from selling a larger quantity at a lower price. In the absence of a monopoly, competitors prevent the emergence of a monopoly price by offering larger quantities for sale at lower prices. However, the existence of a monopoly does not always permit the emergence of monopoly prices since the higher price often reduces net proceeds, as well as sales. Monopoly prices yield monopoly gains—not profits. See "Entrepreneurial profit and loss." Monopoly prices are usually, but not necessarily always, the result of interventionism (q.v.).

   HA. 278, 357-379, 383-387, 680-681, 766-767; OG. 70-78, 248; also PLG. 94-95.

Montaigne dogma.   The dogma of the French essayist, Michel Eyquem de Montaigne (1533-1592) that the gain of one man is the loss of another and that no man makes a profit except at the expense of another. He also held that the same principle applied to trade between nations.

Morbific.   Causing or producing disease.

Mutatis mutandis, (Latin).   The necessary changes being made; with due alteration of details.

N

Nabob. Formerly, a provincial governor or viceroy who lived luxuriously in India. Later, an Englishman who returned wealthy from a tour of duty in India. Hence, any very rich man who lives luxuriously.

National Recovery Administration (1933-1936). The United States Governmental agency charged with the administration of the National Industrial Recovery Act (1933). This was one of the basic acts of the New Deal (q.v.). This Act required the representatives of the employers and employees of every industry to draw up a code of "fair practices" for approval and enforcement by the NRA. These codes provided for Federal Government control of prices, wages, working conditions and trade practices. The Supreme Court declared the Act unconstitutional in May 1935. The provisions regulating employer-employee relations were then rewritten in the (Wagner) National Labor Relations Act (1935), which was subsequently held to be constitutional (1937).

B. 5; also PLG. 241-244.

National socialism. A system of socialism which seeks a specially privileged position for the members of a definite nation. The pre-World War II German National Socialist Party aimed at a socialist organization of the world in which the people of "pure German blood" would be assigned a privileged position, while members of the "inferior" races would be assigned tasks where they would serve the "master (German) race." See "Socialism," "Nazi" and "Socialism of the German pattern."

HA. 323-326; OG. 222-224; S. 578-582.

Natural law, or **the laws of nature.** These terms are used in two senses: (1) The inflexible regularities of the physical and biological phenomena which form the subject matter of the sciences of physics, chemistry, medicine and biology. The actions of men are restricted and conditioned by these laws and thus a knowledge of them is necessary for successful action. (2) The idea that there is an arbitrary eternal standard for determining which human actions are just and therefore beneficial to society and which are not. Many Scholastics (see "Medieval scholasticism") held that natural law was a part of divine law while more recent theorists tend to hold that natural law is a body of rules and customs with which man-made laws should conform for the good of society. Since there is no scientific basis for determining the content of natural law, it is used largely in a vague metaphysical sense and few people agree as to its specific meaning. Consequently, some people resort to the term "natural law" as a justification of social actions or programs they endorse, but which they find themselves unable to define explicitly or defend logically.

   HA. 174-175, 720-721, 761-762, 839; S. 43, 76-77, 319; TH. 44-49.

Natural right. An illusory right supposedly conferred upon individuals by natural law (q.v., sense 2). The emptiness of appealing to any "natural" right becomes evident when an opponent claims a contrary or inconsistent "natural" right. Such differences can only be resolved by resort to sound and effective reasoning.

   HA. 174-175, 285, 720-722, 839.

Natural sciences. Branches of knowledge collectively which deal directly with the phenomena exhibited by natural objects, organic or inorganic, and their substances. There exists among such entities an inexorable regularity in the concatenation and sequence of natural events or physical phenomena. While measurements of such substances may not be precise, they are sufficiently so to permit the use of laboratory experiments and observation for measurements and quantification of knowledge. Sometimes referred to as the physical or empirical sciences, the natural sciences include biology, geology, medicine, physics, chemistry, etc., but not the human sciences, mathematics, philosophy or metaphysics.

   EP. 118-200; HA. 59, 206-207, 637-640, 668n; TH. 90; UF. 6-7, 27, 46, 53-55, 62.

Navicularii, (Latin).   Shipowners.

Nazi, (German).   Short for *Nationalsozialist,* a member of the National Socialist German Workers Party, led to power by Adolf Hitler (1889-1945). Also used as an adjective to signify a connection with the Nazi Party or its policies. Hitler based his absolute dictatorship upon central planning, "Socialism of the German pattern" (q.v.), and his popularity upon appeals to nationalism, anti-Semitism and anticapitalism. The Nazis, under Hitler, ruled Germany from 1933 to the end of World War II in 1945. For the Nazi ideology see *Omnipotent Government,* pages 222-223. Mises then said the Nazi dogmas were those of present-day (1944) " 'unorthodox' orthodoxy," which Fabians and Keynesians were unable to refute. See also "National socialism."

   AC. 109; B. 64, 90, 108; OG. 32, 115, 127, 129-239; PF. 77-78, 141; S. 560, 561, 572, 576, 578-582.

Negative price premium.   See "Price premium."

Neutral money, neutrality of money.   The idea that there is or can be some fixed price structure, or interrelationship of all prices, that is independent of the quantity of money and which therefore is not disturbed by changes in the quantity of money. Adherents of this idea hold that changes in the quantity of money affect the prices of all goods and services proportionally and at the same time. This untenable doctrine is the basis for many attempts to maintain a so-called "stable price level" by manipulating the quantity of monetary units. Actually, all changes in the quantity of money must be introduced by changes in the cash holdings of specific individuals whose purchasing power, value scales and spending patterns are thus altered in a manner which affects different prices differently and sets in motion other price changes as the subsequent recipients of such newly induced spending find their cash holdings increased and they in turn change their spending patterns with differing effects on different goods and services. Thus every change in the quantity of money must affect different prices differently and there can be no such thing as the alleged neutrality of money. See "Quantity theory of money." For other effects of changes in the quantity of money related to the trade cycle, see Chapter XX of *Human Action.*

97

HA. 202, 249, 398-400, 416-422, 541-545; M. 137-145.

Neutral tax. A tax that would collect for the government the funds required for the conduct of public affairs without affecting the mutual relations between individuals or the economic structure of the nation. Such a tax is inconceivable in a market economy where incomes are unequal due to the ever changing data of the market place.

HA. 737-738.

New Deal, American. The program of interventionism (q.v.), social legislation (public works, "social security," etc.) and political expansion of the quantity of money sponsored by the administration of Franklin D. Roosevelt (1882-1945), President of the United States, 1933-1945. This political program, which sought to limit and regulate free market operations while providing subsidies for low income and other important political groups, was considered revolutionary at the time and the Supreme Court declared unconstitutional two of the basic Acts, the National Industrial Recovery Act (1935) (see "National Recovery Administration") and the Agricultural Adjustment Act (1936). However, a shift in Court opinion after the 1936 elections has resulted in decisions which have found almost all forms of subsidies and interventions to be constitutional. See also *Sozialpolitik*.

AC. 65; B. 5; M. 431, 438; OG. 158, 247; PF. 2, 29, 61, 95-96, 98, 103, 136; S. 541, 545, 576; also PLG. 237-246.

Newtonian mechanics. The fundamental laws of the natural sciences (q.v.) as developed from the extraordinary contributions of Sir Isaac Newton (1642-1727), natural scientist, mathematician and philosopher, whose chief work was *Principia* (1687; 2nd edition, 1713).

Nexus. Tie; bond; link; connection or interconnection.

Nominalism. The doctrine that man can only conceive of particular or individual things, persons and events and thus all general or universal terms, such as a tool, a man or a speech, are mere figments of the imagination and non-existing. Opposed to realism, the doctrine that general or universal terms predated particular or individual terms and thus have substantial reality. Nominalists

tend to distrust abstractions and deductive reasoning while leaning on experience and the direct observation of experiments.
   HA. 42; S. 63.

Nominal wage rates. Wage rates in monetary terms without reference to the value of such wages in terms of what they will buy or provide. See "Real wage rates" for contrast.

Nonascetic. Pertaining to those who do not practice asceticism (q.v.).

Non liquet, (Latin). It is not clear or proven; used legally for verdicts deferring a decision in doubtful cases.

Non sequitur, (Latin). Literally, "it does not follow." Given the conditions or situation set forth, a *non sequitur* is a fallacy, illogical inference or unwarranted conclusion.

Nonspecific factor of production. A factor of production (q.v.) which has equal values in the production processes of more than one particular type of economic good or service and is thus capable of alternate uses, as opposed to specific factors of production (q.v.). Examples of nonspecific factors of production are unskilled labor and such raw materials as iron ore and raw cotton.

Normans. Successors to the Vikings (q.v.) who seized and settled in Normandy (area NW of Paris, France, bordering on the English channel) in the ninth and tenth centuries. Their name is derived from Northmen or Norsemen, terms then used for Scandinavians. They adopted Christianity and the French language before undertaking conquests in England, Sicily, parts of Italy and France. Once victorious, the Normans established law and order, while accepting many of the customs of the countries they conquered. In Sicily and southern Italy, they took the part of the downtrodden Christians against their Saracen masters. The best known Norman was William II (1027-1087), Duke of Normandy and a pretender to the English throne. On the death of Edward the Confessor (1002-1066), he invaded England with the Pope's approval and defeated King Harold II in the Battle of Hastings (1066). He was crowned King William I of England, and is known as William the Conqueror. Within five years, he conquered all

99

England, established feudalism, granted the lands to his hench-men and installed Normans in all official Church and State positions.

Normative discipline. A branch of learning that has a set of standards or rules of conduct by which to test, judge or evaluate its subject matter, such as ethics, aesthetics, logic and politics.

Nouveaux riches, (French, pl.). Those who have recently become rich.

Numeraire. An abstract unit of account in a system of social accounting advocated by certain monetary reformers who have held that its use in place of money would provide a perfectly neutral medium for recording exchanges and one which would have no effect on the exchange ratios of market transactions. The concept of such a numeraire is illusory and its employment in economic thinking is misleading.

HA. 186, 249, 418; M. 94.

O

Obfuscated. Darkened or cast in the shadow or background; obscured by withholding proper light or emphasis; hence, confused, bewildered or lost sight of.

Objective use-value. The importance attached to a thing because of its technological capacity to produce chemically or physically a desired effect. An example would be the "heating value" or "heating power" of coal.
HA. 120-121, 127.

Obversion. Transformation by logical inference of a proposition into an equivalent negative, contradictory or obverse proposition, as by inferring from the proposition, "all dogs have heads," that "no dogs are headless."

Oligarchy. Rule by a few or a small exclusive group.

Oligopoly, oligopolist. Literally, few sellers; a market situation in which a few individuals or business organizations own or control the total supply of a given commodity or service. An oligopolist is one of the few who own or control such a total supply.

Omnipotence. The state or quality of being almighty, all powerful, irresistible, able to overcome all opposition to the actor's will, including that of natural laws.
HA. 69-70.

Omnipresent. Present everywhere at the same time.

Omniscience. The state or quality of knowing everything. Omniscience is forever denied to human beings.
HA. 68, 70; UF. 35.

Ontology. The science of being or reality in the abstract, particularly as related to ideas or theories.

Optimum returns, law of. See "Returns, law of," of which it is a part.

Originary interest. The inherent component of gross or market interest rates which represents the ever fluctuating ratio between the values assigned to want satisfactions in the immediate future and those assigned to want satisfactions in the more distant future. In short, the difference between the present values of present and future goods. In addition to the originary interest component, gross or market interest includes the entrepreneurial component (uncertainty of repayment) and the price premium component (anticipated changes in the future values of the particular goods, including the monetary unit, under consideration). For Mises' detailed critical analysis of Böhm-Bawerk's interest theories, referred to in *Human Action,* p. 488n., see below pp. 150ff.
    HA. 237, 430, 524-532, 534-551, 643; M. 349-364; OG. 251.

Oxford (University). Founded early in the twelfth century, Oxford University and its rival, Cambridge University, are the two oldest and most revered universities of Great Britain.

P

Panphysicalism. The theory that holds that all human ideas and acts are determined by physical laws; "that the procedures of physics are the only scientific method of all branches of science. It denies that any essential differences exist between the natural sciences and the sciences of human action."

HA. 18, 23-27; TH. 243; UF. v, 22, 39.

Panslavism. A nineteenth century nationalist movement of various Slavonic groups who resented their political rule by, and economic subservience to, the German and Magyar nobility. The movement envisioned the creation of a federal government of all Slavonic nations, under which the land would be divided equally among the peasants who would elect their local governments. It reached its height in the Revolutions of 1848, after which it subsided into a literary movement to which Russian autocrats appealed in their attempts to extend Russian influence and absolutism into Eastern Europe and the Balkans. One of the main obstacles in the realization of the Panslav program was the Russian oppression of the Poles. Another difficulty was the religious conflict between those who acknowledged the supremacy of the Pope and those who belonged to the Greek Orthodox Church.

Par, Parity. In reference to a monetary unit, par or parity is the amount of precious metal, gold or silver, which has been officially designated as the legal equivalence of the monetary unit.

In reference to foreign exchange, par or parity is the official or established ratio between the amount of a precious metal, usually gold, which is the legal equivalent of the monetary unit of one country and the amount of the same precious metal which is the legal equivalent of the monetary unit of another country. For example, the British pound sterling in 1949 was legally defined as the equivalent of 2.8 times the amount of gold that was the then legal equivalent of the American dollar. So the par or parity for the pound sterling was then stated as $2.80.

Paralogism. Faulty reasoning. In formal logic, a fallacy in which the conclusion does not follow from the premises.

Parameter. In equations, an arbitrary constant quantity which can have different values in otherwise similar equations. An example would be the "time parameter," an arbitrarily selected time period which must remain constant for any one set of simultaneous equations; but which may be varied for other sets of similar equations. In uses other than in equations, parameter has different meanings which have no reference to "mathematical economics."

Pariahs, class of. Members of a very low caste, in the former caste systems of Burma and India, usually relegated to the least desirable occupations such as domestic servants and hired farm hands. The term has become a synonym for outcasts who are excluded from normal social activities.

Parvenus, (French). Upstarts; those newly risen in position, prominence or wealth, frequently by chance or good luck.

Pasha, (Turkish). High rank Turkish official who represented the Sultan's temporal power in a specified area. Formerly, a prince of the blood but later applied as a title after the names of all higher civil and military officials.

Pathological. Due to, or related to, disease.

Pathology. The science of diseases and their medical treatment; the totality of knowledge concerning diseases including their origins, progress, consequences and cures.

Patrie, (French). Native land; fatherland.

Patronus, (Latin). The former master of a freed slave who was still entitled to receive some services from his former slave, for whom he continued to serve as a sort of paternal advisor, protector and defender.

Peculium, (Latin). Originally the savings or property held by a Roman slave by permission of his master. Later, it often included a share of his production and was protected by law. Slaves often used their *peculium* to buy their freedom from their master.

Peel's Act of 1844. The British Bank Charter Act, named after

104

its sponsor and political leader of the Currency School (q.v.), the first lord of the treasury and prime minister, Sir Robert Peel (1788-1850). The Act regulated the operation of the then privately owned Bank of England until World War I. The Bank was divided into two separate departments, one for note issue and the other for deposit banking operations. Further increases in the note issue were limited to those issued against gold deposits. This provision, which prevented the further issue of fiduciary media in the form of banknotes, was suspended three times (1847, 1857 and 1866) before World War I (1914-1918). The gold requirements did not apply to the Banking Department which greatly expanded its deposits against bank loans and thus thwarted the efforts of the Currency School to prevent further credit expansion (q.v.).

HA. 571-572; M. 368-373.

Pendant. Counterpart or parallel; something attached to or connected with.

Penury. Extreme poverty or economic hardship.

Per analogiam, (Latin). By analogy.

Periphrastic. Using a phrase with more words than necessary for a simple direct expression; tending to expression in a drawn out roundabout manner.

Perorate. To harangue or expound at length; to conclude or sum up a long discourse.

Phalanstère, Fourier's, (French). Phalanstery. In the complicated visionary socialist system of François-Marie-Charles Fourier (1772-1837), the phalansteries are the common organizations of essentially self-sufficient cooperative communities. He would permit some inter-phalanstery exchanges between those in different parts of the world. In such communities, all participants would seek their happiness in the abandonment of the restraints normally imposed by the previously existing societies. Minimum subsistence would be a first lien on total production. After that, the balance would be allocated 5/12ths for labor, 4/12ths for capital and 3/12ths for talent. It was assumed that all tasks, even the most menial, could be made sufficiently attractive so that enough workers would always volunteer to perform all necessary communal work.

Pharisaic. Pertaining to the Pharisees, a school of ancient Jews noted for their strict and formal observance of both written law and traditional rites. Hence, tending to observe external forms without regard for the essence of inner spiritual feeling. Thus, a connotation of overly formal, hypocritical self-righteousness.

Phlogiston theory. A chemical theory of fire that was generally accepted for about a century, until disproved in 1775 by Antoine Laurent Lavoisier (1743-1794).

Physiocracy. An early (eighteenth century) economic theory prevalent in France which considered agriculture the prime source of wealth and both manufacturing and trade as sterile. It held that the function of government was to give effect to "natural law." Their maxim, *laissez faire, laissez passer,* gave impetus to free enterprise ideas.

Physiology. That section of the science of biology which deals solely with the operation of the functional processes of the many coordinated physical units of the healthy body. It is not specifically concerned with the mental content of the mind or with mental processes in so far as they are separate from the purely physical processes.

Pied piper. One who uses his ability to attract others in order to lure them to their destruction. The term comes from the Legend of the Pied Piper of Hamelin (Germany) made famous by a poem of Robert Browning (1812-1889). According to the myth, a colorful piper agreed to rid the town of rats for a fee. He played a tune which lured the rats into the river where they drowned. When his fee went unpaid, he played a tune which lured the town's children into a cave from which they never returned.

Plain state of rest. The condition where there is a cessation of all market transactions because, for the time being, no potential buyers or sellers believe they could improve their conditions by further transactions at quoted prices. This is a temporary period that disappears as soon as such conditions disappear.

Pleonasm. An expression which, if omitted, would not change the meaning. Its use is usually considered a fault, but is sometimes acceptable for emphasis.

Pluralis gloriosus, (Latin). Literally, glorious plural. Hence, the use of plural "we" in a manner whereby the user implies a false personal identity of himself with famous or distinguished persons. Example: an Italian boor says, "*We* are the world's greatest painters."

Pluralis imperialis, (Latin). Literally, imperial plural. Hence, the use of the plural "we" in a manner whereby the user implies a false personal identity of himself with the ruling powers of his government. Example: a Britisher, between 1790 and 1945, said, "*We* are ruling India."

Pluralis logicus, (Latin). Literally, logical plural. Hence, the use of the plural "we" for a combination of persons who have a logical identity.

Pluralis majestaticus, (Latin). Literally, majestic plural. Hence, the use of the plural "we" by a monarch speaking in his official capacity in much the same manner as an editor uses the editorial "we."

Plutodemocracy. A term of disparagement which advocates of a socialist dictatorship apply to the democratic regimes of civilized nations. It implies that such nations are ruled by a clique of rich exploiters.

Polylogism. In short, many logics. The theory that the logical structure of the human mind differs according to certain divisions of mankind and that as a result the ideas and logic of men also differ in accordance with the specified classification of men. Marxian polylogism asserts there are differences according to social classes. Others claim there are differences according to race, religion, nationality, etc.

HA. 75-89; OG. 143-147; TH. 31-32, 122-142.

Portent. Forewarning of something to be feared; hint or indication of a future undesired event or consequence.

Positive laws. Man-made laws; laws enacted or recognized (common law) by an established government, including both statutory and judicial law. The term is often used in contrast to natural law (q.v., sense 2) or concepts of imagined ideal or perfect laws.

Positive price premium. See "Price premium."

Positivism. A doctrine taught by Auguste Comte (1798-1857). It holds that man's knowledge of all subjects passes through three stages (theological, metaphysical and positive). Contemporary positivism seeks to apply the experimental methods of the natural sciences (q.v.) to the study of the problems of human action (q.v.). The maxim of positivists is that science is measurement.

   HA. 4, 17-18, 26, 31, 56; TH. 240-250, 285; UF. 36-39, 48-49, 54, 63, 116, 118-120, 122-123.

Postulate. An underlying assumption accepted as true, *a priori,* but acknowledged as indemonstrable because of the limitations of human knowledge or the human mind.

Pound sterling, (£ for *libra,* Latin for "pound"). The monetary unit of the United Kingdom, composed of 20 shillings (s.) of 12 pence (d. for *denarii,* Latin for "pence") each. At one time, the British monetary unit was a troy pound of silver, which became known as a pound sterling. The term sterling stems from "Easterlings," the name given to North German merchants who established a Hansa, or trade guild, in England in the thirteenth century. Their coins were noted for their uniform reliability as to weight and fineness.

   During most of the eighteenth century, England was legally on a bimetallic standard which overvalued silver. As the result of Gresham's law (q.v.), it was in fact on the gold standard. The one pound coin then became the gold sovereign, so called because the King's bust appeared on its face. During the Napoleonic Wars the British Government resorted to credit expansion (q.v.) with the result that the Bank of England suspended the gold redemption of its Notes from 1797 to 1821. The gold standard was legally adopted in 1816 and went into effect in 1821.

   From 1821 until the outbreak of World War I in 1914, the Bank's Notes and gold sovereigns were interchangeable except for short suspensions in 1847, 1857 and 1866. The gold standard was again resumed in 1925 at the pre-war parity rate of $4.86, or .2568 troy ounces of gold, for one paper pound. In 1931 the gold standard was dropped and the value of the pound fell to $3.27 by the end of 1932. The American devaluation of 1933-1934 raised its dollar value to $5.15, but its value continued to fall until 1940 when it was officially declared to be worth $4.03. In 1949, it was further devalued to $2.80, or .08 troy ounces of gold, for one pound sterling. The pound has since been further devalued and is no longer officially tied to gold.

In 1971, the decimal system was adopted and the pound was then subdivided into 100 new pence.

See "Guinea."

Pragmatism. The theory that ideas or principles are true so far as they work. In general, pragmatists rely on empirical or experimental methods and reject apriorism as a source of human knowledge. Because pragmatists differ among themselves in their use of the term, it is difficult to give a short precise definition. For adequate treatment see Dagobert A. Runes' *Dictionary of Philosophy*.

HA. 23-24, 32.

Praxeology, (from the Greek, *Praxis,* action, habit or practice; *logia,* doctrine, theory or science). The science or general theory of (conscious or purposeful) human action. Mises defines action as "the manifestation of a man's will." Accordingly, he considers the use of the adjectives "conscious or purposeful" to be redundant. Praxeology is a manifestation of the human mind and deals with the actions open to men for the attainment of their chosen ends. Praxeology starts from the *a priori* category of action and then develops the full implications of such action. Praxeology aims at knowledge valid for all instances in which the conditions exactly correspond to those implied in its assumptions and inferences. Its statements and propositions are not derived from experience, but are antecedent to any comprehension of historical facts.

EP. (Praxeology translated as "sociology"), viii, 68-124; HA. 1-3, 30-36, 47, 51, 57, 64-71, 174, 646, 648, 651; UF. 14, 41-45, 64-65, 70-72.

Prerogative. A right or privilege which belongs to a person or legal entity by virtue of his rank, office, position or special characteristic which entitles him to precedence or the exercise of some power or advantage not granted to others.

Price level. A confused concept which implies that all prices

109

rise and fall uniformly with changes in the quantity of money or the total of goods and services offered for sale, somewhat as the level of a liquid rises and falls with changes in its quantity or the size of its container. Actually, the term "price level" usually refers to an average of selected prices which individually move quite differently from each other and their average. Acting men are more interested in the interrelationship of different prices than in the movement of all or average prices. When all, or almost all, prices move in the same direction, it is usually a sign of inflation (q.v.) or deflation (q.v.). Continued use of the term "price level" frequently leads to the notion of the neutrality of money (q.v.).

HA. 219-223, 398-401, 408-422; M. 137-145, 188-194.

Price premium. The reflection of anticipated future price changes contained in market interest rates. The component in gross market interest rates which attempts to allow for the anticipated changes in the purchasing power of money, i.e., prices. Because changes in the quantity of money usually precede their effects, the price premium tends to lag behind changes in purchasing power. The price premium is added to, or subtracted from, the originary rate of interest and is one reason for the spread between the originary and market interest rates.

The price premium is *negative* (a minus component) when it reflects an anticipated rise in the purchasing power of money, i.e., a drop in prices, and *positive* (a plus component) when it reflects an anticipated drop in the purchasing power of money, i.e., a rise in prices, as is frequently the case when inflation is anticipated.

HA. 431, 469, 541-545, 547-548, 550-558.

Primordial. Primary; fundamental; rudimentary; elemental; original; existing from the beginning.

Principle of Fullarton. See "Banking School."

Pro anno, (Latin). For a year; annually; *per annum.*

Procrustean. Imposing stern and inflexible conformity to a preconceived theory or system. It originated from the mythical legend of Procrustes who was reputed to tie his victims to an iron bed and then stretch them or cut off their legs to make them fit the bed.

110

Productivity theory of interest. The theory, disproved by Eugen von Böhm-Bawerk (1851-1914) that interest is the income attributed to, or derived from, the use of capital goods in the production process. For the correct theory of interest, time preference, see "Originary interest."

Profit. The goal of every contemplated action (anticipated profit) or the gain or satisfaction derived from every successfully completed action (achieved profit). Since all men prefer success over failure and a greater success over a lesser success, every human action is aimed at obtaining as high a gain or satisfaction (profit) as possible. The opposite of profits is losses, the result of unsuccessful actions, which all human actions seek to avoid or minimize. Both anticipated and achieved profits are of two types, psychic (mental) profit (q.v.) and entrepreneurial (business) profit (q.v.).

   AC. 48, 86; B. 20-39, 64-69, 88, 122-123; HA. 97-98, 239-243, 289-301, 350, 396, 424-425, 534-536, 637, 664-666, 705, 746, 808-811, 827, 871; OG. 102; PF. 108-150.

Progenitive. Able to reproduce.

Progenitor. Parent; founder of a family; ancestor.

Progeny. Children; offspring; descendants.

Progressing economy. An economy in which the per capita quota of invested capital is increasing. This increase in capital goods results in an increase in per capita income. In a progressing economy total entrepreneurial profits thus exceed total entrepreneurial losses. Since incomes and capital accumulation are incapable of measurement, the existence of a progressing economy can only be grasped by resorting to historical understanding.

   HA. 251, 294-300, 414-415; PF. 123-125.

Progressive taxation. A method of taxation under which the tax rate increases as the amount to be taxed increases. It represents an attempt to make wealthy persons pay more than a proportional share of taxes levied on incomes and inheritances. The *Communist Manifesto* (q.v.) endorses progressive taxation as one of ten measures that may be used for effecting "despotic inroads on the rights of property, and . . . as a means of entirely revolutionizing" the social order.

   See PLG. 54-56, 61-62.

111

Proletarian. A wage earner, manual worker or peasant, whom socialists view as one without property and thus, under capitalism, at the mercy of employers. Proletarians are to be distinguished from: (1) The bourgeois or merchants, employers and white collar workers, and (2) The nobility and landed gentry.

AC. 68-70.

Proliferation. Rapid reproduction, multiplication or growth in numbers.

Prophylactics. That part of medical science related to the prevention of, or defense against, disease.

Propitious. Favorable or conducive to success; offering advantageous conditions or circumstances.

Protectionism. The policy of imposing legal burdens or restrictions on imports with the intention of hampering or preventing their competition with domestic products. It includes the use of embargoes, tariffs, import quotas, burdensome import regulations, foreign exchange controls, etc. A protective tariff, unlike a tariff for revenue, is designed to keep out imports rather than raise revenue.

HA. 161-164, 315-318, 509-510, 745, 749-755; OG. 66-69, 75, 244-245, 249-251, 285.

Provenance. Source, origin or derivation, particularly as related to place or persons responsible for the discovery or original production.

Psychic profit and loss. An increase (profit) or decrease (loss) in the acting man's satisfaction or happiness. Psychic profits and losses are sensible, subjective, mental and purely personal. They can be neither measured nor weighed. They can only be felt or sensed. The psychic profit or loss derived from any action can be compared with that of another solely in terms of more or less.

HA. 97, 204-205, 289-290; also PLG. 49-51, 54, 69-71.

Psychology. Psychology is concerned with the minds of men. It has two major meanings. The sciences of human action are not primarily concerned with the physiological meaning, sometimes known as natural or experimental psychology. Whenever Mises refers to psychology in economic studies, he has in mind what some call "literary psychology" and which he has called *"Thymology"* in *Theory and History* and *The Ultimate Foundation of*

Economic Science. In this sense, psychology "is on the one hand an offshoot of introspection and on the other a precipitate of historical experience. It is what everybody learns from intercourse with his fellows. It is what a man knows about the way in which people value different conditions, about their wishes and desires and their plans to realize these wishes and desires. It is the knowledge of the social environment in which a man lives and acts."

It signifies the cognition of human ideas, emotions, volitions, motivations and value judgments which are an indispensable faculty of everyone. It is the specific understanding of the past which gives men an insight into the minds of other men. Psychology, like economics, starts with the individual. It concerns the internal invisible and intangible events of the mind which determine man's value scales which result or can result in action. Economics begins at the point psychology leaves off.

EP. 3, 152-155, 183-202; HA. v, 12, 123-127, 486-488; OG. 230; TH. 264-284; UF. 47-48.

Psychopath. A person with a mental disease, usually characterized by a mental or emotional instability, due to a defect in character or personality, that approaches but falls short of insanity.

Psychopathology. The branch of psychological knowledge that is concerned with mental diseases and disorders.

Psychophysics. The division of psychology that studies the physiological aspects of mental phenomena and in particular the quantitative relations between stimuli and the resultant sensations.

"Pump-priming." Deficit spending by a government on public works and "welfare" projects in an attempt to raise the purchasing power of the recipients and thus stimulate and revive economic activity to the point that deficit spending will no longer be considered necessary to maintain the desired economic activity. "Pump-priming" sometimes fails to catch on, as in the case of the American New Deal of the 1930's. At other times, it starts a boom which inevitably leads to a recession, depression or "flight into real values" (q.v.). See also "Trade cycle" and "Monetary theory of the trade cycle."

HA. 555; also PLG. 237-241.

113

Q

Qua, (Latin).   Considered as; in the capacity or character of; as far as; as.

Quadragesimo anno, (Latin).   In the fortieth year, being the first words of the 1931 encyclical of Pope Pius XI (1857-1939; Pope, 1922-1939). This encyclical refers to and amplifies the *Rerum Novarum* (on new things) encyclical promulgated by Pope Leo XIII (1810-1903; Pope, 1878-1903) forty years earlier (1891). Taken together, these two encyclicals present the official position of the Roman Catholic Church on the social order, including socialism and capitalism.
   S. 255, 429, 577.

Qualitative credit control.   An attempt to force available quantities of credit into specific types of loans, considered desirable, by prohibiting or limiting loans of other types, considered undesirable.

Qualitative economics.   Economic theory based on the knowledge that there are no constant relations in the sphere of human actions and that the exact future is always uncertain because the value judgments of acting men cannot be determined in advance with certainty.
   EP. 116-118; HA. 55.

Quantitative economics.   The theories of "mathematical economists" based on the idea that there are constant relations in the sphere of human actions that can be quantified or measured, thus permitting the application of statistics and mathematical theories to economics. Mises maintains: "There is no such thing as quantitative economics." All statistics are history, sometimes economic history, but never economics (q.v.). See "Mathematical economics."

EP. 116-118; HA. 55-56, 118, 350-357; UF. 62.

Quantity theory of money. Simply stated: The theory that changes in the quantity of monetary units tend to affect the purchasing power of money inversely, that is, with every increase in the quantity of money, each monetary unit tends to buy a smaller quantity of goods and services while a decrease in the quantity of monetary units has the opposite effect. Knowledge of the effects of changes in the quantity of money is vital to an understanding of the theory of money, one of the most misunderstood economic problems of our age.

In 1568, Jean Bodin (1530-1596) pointed out that one reason for the then-recent rise in prices was the greater abundance of money due to the discovery of silver in America. He reasoned that since an abundance of anything made its value fall, this was what had happened in the case of money. In 1588, Bernardo Davanzati (1529-1606) espoused the first crude quantity theory of money by equating the total quantity of monetary metal to the total of all things able to satisfy human wants and then reasoning that the prices of available commodity units were proportional to the available quantity of monetary units. Later versions of this crude theory equated the quantity of money available or the quantity of money that changed hands (quantity × velocity), to the quantity of goods and services exchanged for money and maintained that changes on the money side of the equation resulted in proportional changes in the prices of all goods and services sold, i.e., a 20% increase in the quantity of money, or the quantity of money spent for goods and services would raise all prices proportionally by 20%. See "Equation of exchange."

The fallacy of all such crude versions of the quantity theory is their holistic (see "Holism") viewpoint of market transactions which ignores the fact that all changes in the quantity of money must start with changes in the cash holdings of some specific individuals and that it is through their subsequent market actions that the changes in the quantity of money set in motion their effect on price changes.

The refined and logically unassailable quantity theory of money traces the effect of every change in the quantity of money from its inception, as a change in the cash holdings of certain individuals, through the chain of changes in the prices these individuals pay and the effects such changes produce in the cash holdings and subsequent expenditures of other individuals until the full effect of the change in the quantity of money has spent its force and produced an entirely different set of price ratios or relations (price structures). Although a change in the quantity of money may eventually affect all prices, it does not and cannot affect all prices in the same manner, to the same degree or at the same time. The holistic idea that it does is false and has serious consequences.

See "Monetary theory of the trade cycle," "Money relation" and "Neutrality of money."

HA. 38, 55, 231, 405; M. 115-131, 137-154; also PLG. 146-147, 164-165, 282-283.

R

Rajah, (Hindu). A Hindu chief, or prince, who ruled a territory, either independently or as a feudal lord owing allegiance to an overlord.

Rate of profit. An absurd expression based on the false assumption that there exists a relationship between profit (q.v.) and capital (q.v.). Profits are earned by superior foresight in adapting production to meet future shifts in consumer demand before competitors are aware of the need for such adaptation. Since profits cannot be related mathematically to superior foresight, there can be no meaningful "rate of profit."

Ratiocination. The mental process of reasoning or exact thinking with the implication of an extended process that passes through a number of steps before arriving at the logical conclusion.

Rational. Arrived at by the use of the peculiarly human mental processes by which man strives to connect his ideas as consciously, coherently and purposively as possible in order to plan the attainment of ends sought. In view of the human fallibility in selecting the best possible reasoning for attaining the ends sought, there is no implication as to the correctness or incorrectness of the reasoning. Consequently, all conscious human actions, whether or not appropriate for the ends sought, are rational.

EP. 31-35, 62-66, 135, 148; HA. 19-22, 89-91, 102-104, 177-178, 884; OG. 112-113; also PLG. 13-14.

Rationalism, eighteenth century. The fundamental thesis of rationalism is that man's actions are guided by reason. In the eighteenth century a growing movement stressed the use of reason to expose the fallacies of the myths, superstitions and witch burning of earlier times. The weakness of the movement was the false assumption that all men possessed the same reasoning capacity and thus any disagreement with generally accepted doctrines and ideologies was the result of willful deceit.

HA. 16, 146; TH. 269-270.

Rationalization. The substitution of a rational pretext for a real reason, with an implication of self-delusion or hypocrisy; the improvisation of a plausible reason for a human action when one either does not realize the real reason or seeks to keep it secret; the use of a false but reasonable justification or interpretation of an attitude or action, which appears to be unsatisfactory or contrary to accepted reasoning, when one is either ashamed or not aware of his actual motive.

HA. 78-79; TH. 280-282.

Realism. See "Nominalism."

Realpolitik, (German). Practical politics, in the sense that ideas and theories are unimportant and can be disregarded in the conduct of political affairs. The exponents of *Realpolitik* were unaware of the fact that their own power was also based on ideas and theories.

Real wage rates. Wage rates in terms of what they will buy or provide rather than in terms of monetary units whose purchasing power fluctuates. Real wages also take into account any non-monetary advantages, disadvantages or withholdings that accompany the employment. See "Nominal wage rates" for contrast.

Reclusion. The seclusion of a hermit, recluse or anchorite (q.v.).

Refractory. Rebellious; stubborn; actively resisting.

Regression theorem. The theorem by which Mises applies the subjective theory of value to the objective-exchange value, or purchasing power of money. Objective-exchange values of all other goods and services are explained by the subjective theory of value, whereby the values are traced to the ultimate subjective-use values of the marginal consumers who value such goods and services for their objective-use values which they expect to consume. This is not true for money because (1) money is not consumed in its use and (2) the subjective and objective use values of money coincide and are equal to its objective-exchange value, the estimated value of the goods and services for which it can be exchanged. Mises explains the origin of the objective-use value of money by tracing it back step by step from the point at which it is being valued to the point where the monetary good served only non-monetary uses, an essential point preceding the first use of anything as money. At this point, its objective-exchange value is explained by the general theory of subjective value and marginal utility.

HA. 408-411, 426, 610-611; M. 97-123; also PLG. 141-167. See also Murray N. Rothbard's *Man, Economy and State* (Princeton, N. J.: Van Nostrand, 1962; Los Angeles: Nash Publishing, 1970).

Regressus in infinitum, (Latin). Process of going back endlessly, i.e., tracing each happening to a preceding step.

Reichsbank. The central bank (q.v.) of Germany from 1875 until shortly after World War II.

HA. 552, 570; M. 55-56; PF. 81-82.

Reichswirtschaftsministerium, (German). German Government's Ministry of National Economy.

B. 64; PF. 77.

Relevance, judgments of. See "Judgment of relevance."

Relicta civitate rus habitare maluerit, (Latin). Deserted the cities, preferring to live in the country.

Renitent. Actively resisting; persistently opposed; recalcitrant; struggling in opposition.

Res extra commercium, (Latin). Thing or things outside of business or commercial transactions.

Retrogressing economy. An economy in which the per capita quota of invested capital is decreasing. This decrease in, or consumption of, capital goods results in a decrease in per capita real income. In a retrogressing economy total entrepreneurial losses will exceed total entrepreneurial profits. Since incomes and capital accumulation are incapable of measurement, the existence of a retrogressing economy can only be grasped by resorting to historical understanding.

HA. 251, 294-299; PF. 123-125.

Retrospection.   The act or faculty of looking back on the past.

Returns, law of.   The law of returns provides that for the production of every economic good there is an optimum combination (or proportion) of the required factors of production (q.v.).

It also provides that in those cases where the desired economic good can be produced by other than the optimum combination, all factors but one remaining constant, increasing deviations in the quantities of the variable factor from the optimum quantity will produce proportional or greater than proportional decreases in the returns per unit of the variable factor (Law of diminishing or decreasing returns), while decreasing deviations in the quantities of the variable factor from the optimum quantity will produce proportional or greater than proportional increases in the returns per unit of the variable factor (Law of increasing returns).

The law of returns, in all its parts, applies equally to all factors of production.

EP. 155; HA. 127-131.

Revolution, American (1776-1783).   After repeated attempts to obtain the rights of freemen, representative government, and relief from the discriminatory taxes and despotism of King George III (1738-1820), representatives of the thirteen American colonies, assembled in the Second Continental Congress, declared their independence from England on July 4, 1776. In the subsequent war, the armies of the former colonies, with French help, were able to repulse and finally defeat (1781) the British armies and their mercenaries. The Peace Treaty signed in Paris on September 9, 1783, recognized the full independence of the United States of America.

OG. 237.

Revolution, French (1789-1799).   Violent political upheaval primarily caused by the growing financial difficulties of the absolute

Bourbon Kings of France and the rise of liberal ideas. Faced with financial bankruptcy, King Louis XVI (1754-1793) called the *États-Généraux* (q.v.) to meet on May 1, 1789. The Third Estate (q.v.), refusing to accept one vote out of three, illegally organized itself into a Constituent National Assembly for drafting a constitution which the King was later forced to accept. Meanwhile, Royal troop movements and food shortages led to worker uprisings in Paris and, on July 14, 1789, to the storming of the Bastille prison. The Assembly adopted a Declaration of the Rights of Man, abolished feudal dues and church tithes, while confiscating church property, against which it issued assignats (see *"Mandats territoriaux"*). The clergy were ordered to swear allegiance to the new order which the Pope forbad them to do. This led to domestic disorders at the same time that attempts of foreign royalty to aid the French nobility led to war. Paris masses were aroused against the King who was deposed, tried and beheaded. A newly formed Republic (1792) led to Civil War and a "Reign of Terror" during which those in power constantly murdered all suspected opponents. War, inflation and price controls led to a Revolutionary Government which prepared the way for the rise of Napoleon I (1769-1821) as First Consul (1799) and Emperor (1804). However, feudalism remained abolished.

HA. 286n, 823.

Revolution of 1688, English. An almost bloodless revolution, sometimes called "The Glorious Revolution." It arose as the result of religious conflicts and the King's practice of dispensing with judges and Parliamentary laws that did not meet with his favor. King James II (1633-1701), a Roman Catholic and the last of the absolute English rulers, was forced to flee to France (1688) before Dutch forces that Tory and Whig leaders had asked the Protestant Prince William of Orange to bring to England. A special Parliament offered the throne to William and his wife, Protestant daughter of James II, and they became William III and Mary, joint rulers with powers limited by a Bill of Rights which later became a model for the American Bill of Rights. The revolution marked the ascendancy of the House of Commons over the House of Lords as well as the rise to power of the Whig Party over the Tory Party. It also marked the beginning of cabinet government, independence of judges, regular meetings of Parliament, the freedom of religious worship, Parliamentary budget control of taxes and expenditures and, later (1695), the freedom of the press.

Ricardian.　Pertaining to the theories of the classical economist, David Ricardo (1772-1823). His chief work was *The Principles of Political Economy and Taxation* (1817). Ricardo endorsed the division of labor and social cooperation as beneficial to all (see "Comparative cost, law or theory of"), established the fact that political interference with free trade (tariffs) must curtail consumer satisfaction and that marginal land receives no rent for its use. This last contained the germ for the later developed theory of marginal utility which forms the basis for the subjective-value theory. Ricardo's chief weaknesses were his endorsement of the labor theory of value, the domestic use of fiduciary money, the "Ricardo effect" (q.v.) and the idea that the economic problem is concerned with the distribution of shares of the final product to land, labor and capital.

Ricardo effect, the.　A proposition of David Ricardo (1772-1823) that an increase in wage rates will lead to a replacement of labor by machines and vice versa, an increase in machinery costs will lead to the use of more labor. This proposition is often cited by interventionists who claim that raising wage rates will increase the use of machinery and thus total production. The argument confuses cause and effect; it is the increased use of capital goods that raises wage rates. Unless increased savings become available, any increase in the use of capital goods by one industry merely reduces the quantity of capital goods available for other industries. When interventionism takes the form of higher than market wages in one firm or industry, it merely produces a shift in the use of the available supplies of capital goods. It thus reduces the marginal productivity of both labor and capital and results in a drop in total production and consumer satisfaction, as existing capital is shifted to where it is less productive than in a free or unhampered market.

　　HA. 773-776.

Ricardo's law of association. See "Comparative cost, law or theory of," the better known term. Mises prefers the term, "Ricardo's law of association" because the same principle applies not only to international trade, with which it is usually identified, but also to all other social relations.

Roundabout methods of production. A term devised by the Austrian economist, Eugen von Böhm-Bawerk (1851-1914), to describe the capitalistic production process whereby capital goods are produced first and then, with the help of the capital goods, the desired consumer goods are produced. Since "roundabout methods" imply a circuitous indirectness that is more time consuming than is necessary for the ends sought, Mises stresses the fact that the capitalistic method of production is the shortest, quickest, most direct and most economic method known for attaining the ends sought—greater consumer satisfaction.

HA. 482.

Russian pattern of socialism. See "Socialism of the Russian pattern."

123

S

Sabotage, n. and v.   To injure or destroy willfully and maliciously; from the practice of early French and Belgian workers who threw their sabots (hollowed-out wooden shoes) into machinery they sought to disable due to fear that use of machinery would lead to mass unemployment.

Sane sicut lux se ipsam et tenebras manifestat, sic veritas norma sui et falsi est, (Latin).   A dictum of Spinoza (1632-1677). Translation: "Indeed, just as light defines itself and darkness, so truth sets the standard for itself and falsity."

Scab.   A derogatory term used to signify one who works, or continues to work, at a place of employment against which a union has called a strike.

Schizophrenia.   An abnormal state of mind or mental derangement characterized by distorted views of reality and the presence of conflicting ideas, impulses or emotions which lead to fantastic delusions and a disintegration of personality.

Scholastic philosophy.   See "Medieval scholasticism."

"Scientific" socialism.   See "Socialism, 'scientific.' "

Second International.   A loose federation of national groups of Marxian socialists that was first organized at Paris in 1889, on the 100th anniversary of the French Revolution. It followed about fifteen years after the dissolution of "The International Workingmen's Association" or "The International," now known as "The First International," which was founded at London in 1864, under the domination of Karl Marx (1818-1883). This second attempt to

124

promote international socialist unity disintegrated with the advent of World War I. After the war, many of its components were absorbed into "The Labor and Socialist International" which first met at Hamburg in 1923. Others were absorbed into "The Third (or Communist) International" which first met at Moscow in 1919.

AC. 98; HA. 152; OG. 51, 149, 154, 164-166, 180.

Secular. Long enduring, long term, usually used in contrast to short term. Technically, when used in non-religious terminology, secular implies a duration of several centuries. When used in reference to religion (HA. 527, 587), secular means worldly, nonreligious, outside of the church.

Sedulous. Diligent and persevering; hard working and persistent.

Seigniorage. A charge made for converting monetary metal into coins.

Seven Years' War (1756-1763) An almost world-wide war between England, Prussia and Hanover on one side and France, Austria, Saxony, Russia, Sweden and later (1762) Spain on the other. It involved colonial possessions and the Austro-Prussian conflict for domination over a more united German speaking central Europe. The Peace Treaties of 1763 established British supremacy in India and America and Prussian (Hohenzollern) ascendancy in central Europe. The American phase of this war is generally known as the French and Indian War.

Sine qua non, (Latin). Necessity; requisite; something absolutely necessary or indispensable.

Slavonic Bolsheviks. Eastern European Bolsheviks (q.v.) who speak one of the Slavic languages. These include the Russians, Poles, Czechs, Slovaks, Yugoslavs (Serbs, Croats and Slovenes) and Bulgarians.

Social competition. The striving of individuals to attain the most favorable position in a system of social cooperation.

HA. 273-274; S. 320-321.

Social Democratic Party, German. A German political party which in the late nineteenth century was a leading member group of the Second International (q.v.), the most influential movement for the spread of Marxism, and a model for the Social Democratic parties of other countries. The Party was founded in 1869 by Wilhelm Liebknecht (1826-1900) and August Bebel (1840-1913), devoted advocates of Marxian doctrines, including those of non-compromising class warfare, the inevitable collapse of capitalism and the eventual proletarian seizure of power. In 1874-1875, the Party, in merging with a group of followers of Ferdinand Lasalle (1825-1864), an advocate of socialism by interventionism, adopted the Gotha Program opposed by Karl Marx (1818-1883). From 1878-1890, German law declared the advocacy of socialism to be subversive. All Party meetings and literature were thus banned, but the Party continued to grow at the polls and in members of the Reichstag. In 1891, in adopting the Erfurt Program, the Party reendorsed Marxian doctrines as rewritten by Karl Kautsky (1854-1938). However, the Party in practice drifted into endorsement of the "revisionist" policies of political opportunism and interventionism sponsored by Eduard Bernstein (1850-1932). The Party thus attempted to hold the loyalty of trade union members for which the government was bidding with "social insurance" and other "pro-labor" interventions. In 1912, the Party received one-third of the total Reichstag vote. During World War I, dissension split the Party into two groups: the so-called Majority Socialists, who endorsed the war effort; and the Independents. After the outbreak of the Russian Revolution (1917), a group seceded from the Independents to form the German Communist Party which later joined the Communist International. Between the World Wars, the Social Democratic Party was the largest German political party, although it never succeeded in winning a majority.

In 1933, the Nazis abolished the Social Democratic Party and all other rival parties. Since World War II, the Party has rejected nationalization and sponsored welfare-state-planned-economy policies. It has been the leading rival of the dominant Christian Democratic Union Party.

OG. 51, 149-168, 193-221; PF. 98; S. 83, 543-549, 572; TH. 144.

Socialism.   A system of social organization that calls for the public ownership of the means of production. A policy which aims at constructing a society in which all the material means of production are under the exclusive control of the organized community, i.e., government, the social organism of coercion, compulsion and repression.

Under socialism, the organized community would not only determine what is to be produced, how it is to be produced and who is to produce it, but also who is to receive the products and how they are to be used. Under such a monopolistic ownership and control of the factors of production, there would be no market for such factors and thus no place for a medium of exchange (money) or the use of economic calculation which must be based on market prices. In the final analysis, all decisions would be centralized under one supreme authority. Accordingly, the principles of socialism, if carried to their logical conclusion, would inevitably lead to a one-man dictatorship.

For distinction from communism, see "Communism."

AC. 62-66, 102, 111-112; B. 10, 29-30, 57-59, 92, 99-100, 103, 105, 109, 114-115, 118-119, 123-125; FC. 19, 62, 70-75; HA. 73-74, 183, 205-206, 258-259, 265, 284-285, 565-566, 675-682, 689-715, 716-718, 758-759, 858-861; OG. 51-58, 107-111, 178-180, 267-271, 284-286; PF. 4-5, 19, 24, 149, 163; S. 20, 56, 113-122, 128, 207, 239, 532-553; UF. 99.

Socialism of the German pattern.   An economic system completely planned and controlled by the government while retaining many of the labels and nominal forms of capitalism. A form of socialism (q.v.) which retains the appearance and terminology of the market economy while in fact private ownership of the means of production, real buying and selling, and real market prices, wages and interest rates no longer exist because all production activities and product allocations are directed and controlled by government orders which all participants are bound to obey unconditionally. This form of socialism was put into operation in Germany during the Nazi regime (1933-1945) but collapsed with the German defeat in World War II. The German term is *Zwangswirtschaft* (q.v.), a compulsory economic system. See "Nazi."

HA. 323-325, 474, 691, 717-718, 758-759, 764; OG. 56-58, 203-206; PF. 4-5, 24-25, 75-78; S. 529, 584.

127

Socialism of the Russian pattern. A form of socialism (q.v.) in which all the material means of production (farms, factories, capital goods, stores, etc.) are legally owned by the government and operated by government employees as ordered by government directives. Such a system does not maintain the appearance of market transactions in the means of production as does "Socialism of the German pattern" (q.v.).

B. 87; HA. 717; OG. 55-56; PF. 4; S. 529, 582-589.

Socialism, "scientific" and "utopian." A distinction between "scientific socialism" and "utopian socialism" was one of the basic ideas of Marxism. According to Karl Marx (1818-1883), utopian socialists were those who aimed at demonstrating that conditions in a socialist society would be incomparably more satisfactory than those of existing social conditions. Utopian socialists attempt to bring about the transition to socialism by convincing people that socialism is in every respect more desirable than the system of private ownership of the means of production. Marx rejected such views as fallacious. He asserted that socialism will not come because people may prefer it; but because, as he had discovered and revealed, historical evolution necessarily and inevitably leads to the establishment of socialism. From this viewpoint, Marxian socialists claim the term "scientific" for themselves, while disparaging the older socialist authors as "utopian" dreamers.

B. 57; S. 17, 281, 356; UF. 129.

Social security. Term now generally applied to political programs which provide welfare payments for the benefit of special classes of the population considered to be deserving of special financial assistance.

In 1883, the German Government established a compulsory insurance system for all German employees. This system was designed to replace public relief with a program providing insurance for employee sicknesses, accidents and old age. In the following decades this system abandoned its actuarial basis and became more and more a system of benefits and pensions financed by taxes on wages. The system has been adopted step by step by almost all industrial nations. It was first enacted in the United States in 1935 as part of the New Deal (q.v.) of President Franklin D. Roosevelt.

HA. 367-368, 617, 839, 847-848; PF. 29, 83-93; S. 475-478; TH. 144.

Society. A system of peaceful and purposeful collaboration in the division of labor and the interchange of goods and services for mutual advantage. A joint action of cooperation in which each participant sees the satisfaction of other participants as a means for the attainment of his own satisfaction. A human society requires the services of a government for the suppression of all anti-social actions.

EP. 42-43, 58, 110; HA. 143-176, 195-198; TH. 251-256; UF. 81, 105, 108-109.

Sociology. A term first proposed by Auguste Comte (1798-1857), a French positivist (see "Positivism"), to signify a suggested science that would develop the laws of human development according to the methods employed in the development of man's knowledge of the natural sciences. Most of the writings that are today called sociological deal with various problems which were previously considered as studies in the fields of history, anthropology and ethnology.

EP. viii, 4-5, 17-22, 68-124; HA. 30; TH. 241-242; UF. 39, 101-103.

Sociology of Knowledge. An attempt to salvage the discredited Marxian ideology doctrine which Karl Mannheim (1893-1947) and Max Scheler (1874-1928) inaugurated in the 1920's. As Mannheim admits that there exist "unattached intellectuals" who are fit to grasp truth free from "ideological" distortions, the whole discussion leads into an impasse.

OG. 145; UF. 130.

Solo in un secondo tempo, quando le categorie non abbiano trovato la via dell' accordo e dell' equilibrio, lo Stato potrà intervenire, (Italian). "Only at a later stage, if the guilds *(corporazione)* have not succeeded in reaching an acceptable agreement, will the State be able to intervene." NOTE: The same principle applied to labor-management relations within each industry's guild, to which every member of the industry was legally compelled to belong.

129

Soviet economy, or **system.** Socialism of the Russian pattern (q.v.).

S. 582-589.

Soziale Marktwirtschaft, (German). Literally, social management of the market economy. Actually, Mises refers to the system of economic management adopted by the German Government after World War II. By and large this system embraced the interventionist policies of the United States. In some cases, Germany adopted American methods (e.g. antitrust policies); in other cases, Germany espoused more radical policies (e.g. granting labor unions the right of co-determination in certain key industries); while, in still other cases, Germany remained more "orthodox" (e.g. preferring relatively sound money policies as against inflationism).

Sozialpolitik, (German). Literally, social politics. More specifically, the policies of political intervention launched by the German Chancellor, Prince Otto von Bismarck (1815-1898), in 1881 in an attempt to compete with the Social Democratic Party (q.v.), the party of the Marxist socialists, for the political loyalty of the wage earners. While many of the features of this policy were modelled on British patterns, social security legislation was an institution never before tried. The German *Sozialpolitik* was the forerunner of welfare state policies in Europe and of the American New Deal inaugurated in 1933 by Franklin D. Roosevelt (1882-1945). The advocates of such policies deny the existence of economic law and fail to realize that such political interventions result in lower living standards for the very masses they seek to help by so-called "pro-labor" legislation.

B. iv; FC. vi; HA. 367-368, 832-835; OG. 59-66, 76-78, 158-161, 202; PF. 47-48, 96; TH. 144.

Specific factor of production. A "factor of production" (q.v.), which has value in the production process of only one particular type of economic good or service and which is thus valueless for the production of anything else. An example would be a machine for wrapping razor blades which could not be used for anything else.

130

Speculation. Dealing with the uncertain conditions of the unknown future. Every human action is a speculation in that it is embedded in the flux of time.

HA. 58, 112-113, 250, 252-253, 336, 457, 584-585; M. 252-257; S. 205-208, 509; UF. 50-51, 66-67.

Speenhamland system. In February 1793, England went to war with France. The war was financed largely by inflation which, accompanied by poor crops and the Corn Laws (q.v.) raised food prices faster than wages, causing great suffering among workers and their families. In 1795, the magistrates of Berkshire, meeting at Speenhamland, opposing higher minimum wages, adopted a system of using tax revenues to supplement wages to provide workers' families with what they considered a subsistence income. The system spread rapidly to other counties. It resulted in higher incomes for the landed aristocracy, lower wages for workers, less incentives for low paid agricultural workers to shift to higher paying industrial jobs, higher birth rates and constantly rising taxes, until the system was replaced by the Poor Laws of 1834.

Spirochetes. Very slender and spirally bacteria which are the cause of such diseases as yaws, syphilis and recurrent or relapsing fever.

Stalinists. Followers of Joseph Stalin (1879-1953), a poorly educated but ardent and adamant supporter of the Russian Communist Revolution, who resorted to expedient tactics to eliminate Leon Trotsky (1877-1940) and his other more doctrinaire rivals in the contest for the Russian dictatorship upon the death of Nikolai Lenin (1870-1924).

PF. 98; S. 561-566.

Standard coins. Monetary coins which have unlimited legal tender power. Standard coins do not include minor or subsidiary coins which have only limited legal tender power.

Standesherr, (German). A German prince or count whose family was mediatized (q.v.) at the beginning of the nineteenth century. These families then lost the ruling powers they had enjoyed under the Holy Roman Empire. However, they retained certain privileges, properties and the right to marry royalty until the adoption of the Weimar Constitution after World War I.

Ständische Landtage, (German). Territorial assemblies of representatives of the estates of the realm. Starting about the beginning of the fourteenth century, most of the duchies, principalities and kingdoms of the Holy Roman (German) Empire (800-1806) had these diets or assemblies composed of representatives of the three estates, i.e., the nobility, the clergy and the third estate or commons (chiefly the burghers, landowners and lesser aristocrats). These *Landtage* were often important checks on the provincial rulers before the Thirty Years War (1618-1648) which devastated much of Germany, reduced the population by more than one half and reduced the powers of the *Landtage* to assemblies that merely endorsed the wishes of their rulers. However, the *Ständische Landtage* continued to exist as nominal but powerless bodies until the end of the Empire and in a few cases even to the middle of the nineteenth century.

State of rest. See "Final state of rest," "Plain state of rest."

Static equilibrium. Evenly rotating economy (q.v.).
EP. 108; UF. 42.

Stationary economy. The imaginary construction of an economy in which the per capita income and wealth remain unchanged. In such an economy total profits would be precisely equal to total losses. It is only in such an unreal and imaginary economy that the equations of "mathematical economists" would have any validity. See "Mathematical economics."
HA. 250-251, 255-256, 294; PF. 123.

Statism. The doctrine or policy of subordinating the individual unconditionally to a state or government with unlimited powers. Statism includes both socialism (q.v.) and interventionism (q.v.).
B. 74-76, 78; OG. 5, 44-78, 285.

Stato corporativo, (Italian). The corporative state or nation. For program, see "Corporativism."
OG. 178; UF. 130.

Statolatry. Worship of the state. Worship of the state is worship of force.
OG. 46-47.

Sterling area, sterling bloc. Terms applied, ever since Great Britain went off the gold standard in 1931, to those countries which keep large parts of their monetary reserves in "pounds sterling" (q.v.) with the Bank of England in order to maintain the established parity of their monetary units with the (British) pound sterling, rather than gold or silver.

Straiten. Limit, narrow, confine or reduce to the point of creating difficulty or distress.

Strikebreaker. A person employed in the place of one who has left employment because of a strike or concerted work stoppage on the part of a number of workers due to disagreement over wages, working conditions or some particular action or actions of an employer. A strikebreaker differs from a scab (q.v.) in that he may be paid premium wages and is usually hired merely for the duration of a strike rather than for the normal duration of the job.

Subaltern. A person occupying a lower, inferior or subordinate rank or position.

Subjective economics. The general economic theory developed from the subjective-value theory as expounded by the "Austrian School of Economics" (q.v.).

Subjective theory of value. The theory, held by the Austrian economists and by the Anglo-Saxon followers of the English economist, W. Stanley Jevons (1835-1882) and the American economist, John Bates Clark (1847-1938), that the value of economic goods is in the minds of individual men and therefore is neither constant nor inherent in the goods themselves; that values of the same good vary, as the judgments of the individuals making the valuations vary, from person to person and from time to time for the same person. See "Subjective-value theory" and "Marginal theory of value."
EP. 146-181; M. 38-45; also PLG. 27-63.

Subjective use-value. The importance attached to an object or service due to the belief, judgment, knowledge or expectation that its use can produce a desired effect. If it is based on a belief, judgment or expectation, it may or may not be true. Likewise, a thing with the power to produce a desired effect may not have subjective use-value for a person who is not aware of this fact.
HA. 120-121; M. 38-45.

Subjective-value theory. The value theory of the modern economists (the followers of Carl Menger, 1840-1921, W. Stanley Jevons, 1835-1882, and Leon Walras, 1834-1910) which holds that the relative values of goods and services, in the sense that values determine human actions, are to be found in the minds of acting men at the moment of their decisions to act or not to act and not in the physical characteristics or the costs of production of such goods and services. Value is thus said to be subjective rather than objective. See "Marginal theory of value."
EP. 146-181; M. 38-45; OG. 113; also PLG. 27-63.

Subjectivist economics. Economics based on the theory that the value of goods is not inherent in the goods themselves but is in the minds of acting men; that economic value is a matter of individual judgment which may vary from person to person and for the same person from time to time.
EP. 93-97.

Subsidiary coins. Token money (q.v.) in the form of coins for smaller amounts than those of standard coins (q.v.).

Sub specie aeternitatis, (Latin). From the viewpoint or mental image of eternity.

Subtrahendum, (Latin). A thing or quantity to be subtracted.

Sui generis, (Latin). Unique; of a class by itself; of its own kind.

Supererogatory. Superfluous; nonessential; doing something above and beyond what is required by law, duty, custom or normal circumstances.

Supernumerary. Excessive number of; superfluous; a number beyond what is necessary, usual or required.

Sword of Damocles. As told by Cicero (106-43 B.C.), the sword suspended by a single horsehair over the head of Damocles, a courtier invited to dinner by the elder Dionysius (c. 430-367 B.C.) of Syracuse, Sicily, whom Damocles had flattered excessively. Hence, something precarious that is threatening or intimidating.

Sybaritism. The theory that the highest human happiness is to indulge one's sensual desires for rare and luxurious pleasures, such as living the life of a rich and unrestrained royalty.

Sycophant. One who seeks wealth, power or influence from an accepted leader or leaders by undue flattery, adulation or servility.

Syllogisms. A three-part process of deductive reasoning consisting of (1) major premise (usually a general rule), (2) minor premise (usually an individual case employing one term appearing in the major premise) and (3) a conclusion which must follow if both the major and minor premises are true (usually the substitution of the new term of the minor premise in the major premise in place of the term common to both premises). Example:

> Major premise: All dogs are animals
> Minor premise: Betsy is a dog
> Conclusion: Betsy is an animal.

Syndicalism. A naive and impractical proposal for the economic organization of society whereby the workers of each plant, company or economic unit would jointly and equally own and operate the organization for which they work. It supposes the elimination of entrepreneurs and the expropriation of investments so that all "unearned income," i.e., interest and profits, would be equally divided among the workers of each economic unit. Under syndicalism, the incomes of workers doing similar work would vary greatly, depending largely on the wide variation in both the efficiency and the capital invested in the unit by which they were employed.

Syndicalism is also used in the sense of *action directe* (q.v.) wherein it is considered not as a final objective but rather as a means for bringing about socialism.

AC. 109-110; HA. 812-820; S. 270-275; UF. 130.

135

T

Tabula rasa, (Latin).   A clean slate; a blank or erased tablet.

Tabular standard.   A proposed method for the settlement of deferred payments (sums due after the passage of time) wherein the sum due changes in accordance with changes in a standard which is believed to reflect changes in the purchasing power of the monetary unit with the passage of time. The tabular standard specifies a previously agreed upon table which adds the prices for specified quantities of a selected group of commodities as of the date of the agreement and again at the dates that payments are due. The percentage change from the original date is supposed to indicate the change in the purchasing power of the monetary unit during the interim and thus the sum of money which will provide the recipient with the same purchasing power that was contemplated at the time of the original agreement. The proposal lacks scientific precision and at best gives a rough approximation of changes in the purchasing power of the monetary unit during periods of inflation and deflation. See "Index numbers" and "Mathematical economics."

   HA. 222-223, 351, 398-400; M. 201-203, 401-410.

Tantamount.   Equivalent in effect or significance; not differing in essence (from).

Tariff.   A tax, charge or schedule of charges levied upon imports from abroad. See "Protectionism."

Tartars, or **Tatars.**   Nomadic hordes from Central Asia, who, largely under Mongol leadership, overran large parts of Asia and Eastern Europe in the thirteenth century. Their Golden Horde Empire penetrated as far east as Silesia (East Germany) and Hungary. They slaughtered their opponents and lived off the land for more than a century until crushed (1395) by another conqueror, Tamerlane (1336?-1405). Many remained in Siberia, Southern Russia and Turkey.

OG. 237.

Tautology. Repetition of the same idea in different words.
UF. 17.

Technocrat. An advocate of technocracy, an anticapitalistic fallacy that was popular in the depression days of the early 1930's. Technocrats sought their utopia in (1) the abolition of profits, businessmen and market principles, and (2) the establishment of a society run by industrial engineers and other technical experts in accordance with the principles of advanced technology.

Technological unemployment. See "Unemployment, technological."

Teleology. The theory that the cause and direction of changes in phenomena are determined by a previously existing plan or purpose, as opposed to mechanism wherein they are determined according to the laws of the natural sciences (q.v.). All human actions (purposive human behavior) are teleological, i.e., they are activated by the purpose of the actor.

HA. 23-26; UF. 6-8.

Tertium comparationis, (Latin). Literally, a third for comparison. Hence, a basis of comparison.

Theism. In the eighteenth century sense, Theism meant a belief in one God as the Creator and as the Almighty ever present power on earth and in man. Theists in general accepted the teachings of revelation and grace and differed from Deists (see "Deism") in this respect.

Theorem of Pythagoras. The theorem that the square of the hypotenuse of a right-angled triangle is equal to the sum of the squares of the two other sides.

Theory. A theory is an abstract formulation of the constant relations between entities or, what means the same thing, the necessary regularity in the concatenation (q.v.) and sequence of phenomena and/or events. A theory may be true or false. A valid theory attempts to eliminate all contradictions in the application of cause and effect to a given specific situation or set of conditions. The aim of a theory is always success in action. A characteristic of a true theory is that action based on it succeeds in attaining the expected results. A theory is implicit in every human action and likewise a theory necessarily precedes the determination of "facts" and the writing of all history as well as the interpretation of every experience.

EP. vi, xii, xv, 28-31; HA. 646-647; TH. 123, 129; UF. 16; also PLG. 16-20.

Therapeutics.   The part of medical science related to the application of drugs and other remedies for curing or healing disease.

Third Estate (*Tiers État,* French).   The third order or section of the French assembly, *États-Généraux* (q.v.). Originally the Third Estate members were elected by the *bourgeoisie* (q.v.) of the large towns. Later, those of the small towns and rural areas participated in their election. While the Third Estate was spoken of as the representation of the common people, it was elected by tax-paying males aged 25 or over and the proletarians (q.v.) had no voice in the elections. The first two Estates or orders represented the clergy and the nobility. Each Estate met and voted separately. Thus, the Third Estate was unable to end the special privileges of the clergy (compulsory tithes) and the nobility (tax exemptions). The call of the 1789 *États-Généraux* provided the Third Estate with twice as many members as each of the other two Estates. On meeting, the Third Estate insisted the three Estates meet as one body with per capita voting. This was opposed by the King and the leaders of the other two Estates. The Third Estate then organized the Constituent National Assembly with minority members of the other Estates and the French Revolution (see "Revolution, French") ensued abolishing the privileges of the clergy and nobility.

Third Republic in France (1870-1940).   The French government which began with the overthrow of the Second Empire (1852-

1870), following the defeat of Napoleon III (1808-1873) by Germany, and lasted to the French defeat by Germany in 1940. The First Republic lasted from 1792 to 1804, and the Second from 1848 to 1852.

Thymology. See "Psychology."

Token money. Usually minor or subsidiary coins, but actually any distinguishable material which circulates as a substitute for a small amount of money and whose value as money exceeds its commodity value. Token money is generally needed to facilitate exchanges involving small amounts of money and for that reason, its acceptability is often limited to a maximum sum. Token money differs from fiat money (q.v.) in that it is, within limits, a claim for money proper and the amount outstanding is usually limited to the quantity needed for settling small amounts. Token money is a money-substitute (q.v.) and so far as its monetary value exceeds its commodity value, it is a fiduciary medium (q.v.).
HA. 432-433; M. 50-57, 483.

Trade cycle. More popularly, the business cycle. The periodic rhythmical regularity of continuously recurring changes that are assumed to occur in aggregate economic activity. The phases of the trade cycle are loosely: a feverishly booming prosperity which ends in an acute crisis or panic; a period of liquidation, heavy unemployment and adjustment popularly known as a recession or depression; and a revival or recovery period that sets off an upsurge that leads to a new boom.
Karl Marx (1818-1883) originated the idea that recurrent crises are inherent in the unhampered (free) market economy. Mises has shown that "the trade cycle is . . ., on the contrary, the inevitable effect of manipulation of the money market." (*The Freeman*, September 24, 1951. 1(#26):829). See "Monetary theory of the trade cycle."
HA. 571-586.

Transvaluation. A change or shift in valuations.

Triangular trade. A foreign trade situation in which the flow of trade is balanced among three countries, as A exports to B, B exports to C, and C exports to A. The term triangular trade is often used to symbolize the fact that most foreign trade is more complicated than the simple assumption of an even balance of the exports and imports moving between every two countries trading with each other.

Tropism. The involuntary movement of an organism activated by an external stimulus wherein the organism is either attracted to or repelled from the outside stimulating influence. An example is heliotropism, the movement wherein plants turn toward the sun.

Trotskyists. Followers of Leon Trotsky (1877-1940), a Russian intellectual and communist revolutionist with orthodox Marxian ideas who agreed with Joseph Stalin (1879-1953) in all essential matters except as to minor tactics and who should become the Russian dictator upon the death of Nikolai Lenin (1870-1924). Expelled from the Communist Party (1927) and banished from Russia (1929), Trotsky was murdered in Mexico (1940). See "Stalinists."
S. 561-566.

Truman Administration. The United States Presidential Administration (1945-1953) of Harry S. Truman (1884-1972), a former Senator and Vice President, who became President upon the death of Franklin D. Roosevelt (1882-1945). President Truman and his subordinates were strong advocates of further intervention, particularly when prior intervention had created difficulties in employer-employee relations.

Trumpery. Pretentious and misleading; showy but nonsensical; intentionally deceptive.

Truth. The most adequate comprehension of reality that man's mind and reason make accessible to him. Man is fallible and can never become omniscient or absolutely certain that what he considers as certain truth is not error. The criterion of truth is that it works even if nobody is prepared to acknowledge it.
B. 113; HA. 24, 68; UF. 94.

U

Ultima ratio, (Latin). Final reason or argument, which is force.

Understanding. The power of the human mind to grasp or comprehend the significance of a situation faced by men, from the knowledge of given, but incomplete, data not subject to identical repetition. Understanding seeks the meaning of action in intuition of a whole. Understanding takes into account not only given facts but also the reactions of other men, value judgments, the choice of ends and the means to attain such ends and the valuation of the expected outcome of actions undertaken. Understanding is the result of intellectual insight rather than factual knowledge, but it must always be in harmony with (not contradict) the valid teachings of all other branches of knowledge, including those of the natural sciences. Understanding is practiced by everyone and is the only appropriate method for dealing with history and the uncertainty of future conditions, or any other situation where our knowledge is incomplete.

EP. 12, 48, 130-145 (essay title translated "Conception and Understanding"; Mises preferred "Comprehension and Understanding"); HA. 49-59, 68, 112, 118; TH. 310-311; UF. 48-51.

Unearned income. A term which socialists, syndicalists, interventionists and tax authorities apply to rent, interest and entrepreneurial profits. This idea is derived from the early classical or labor theory of value, according to which only labor produces or "earns" increased values.

HA. 396, 772; PF. 122.

Unemployment, catallactic. Unemployment due to the voluntary decision of those unemployed. Given the prevailing market conditions and the personal situations of the unemployed, they prefer not to accept the pay, place, type or other terms of employment open to them. They remain unemployed either because they prefer leisure or because they believe that by waiting they can obtain employment they consider more satisfactory than that available to them at the moment.

HA. 579, 598-602.

Unemployment, frictional. Term sometimes used for certain forms of "Unemployment, catallactic" (q.v.). The term is used by some when the unemployment is assumed to be the result of difficulties in matching job openings and applicants due to certain "frictions" such as lack of information or differences as to skills, training or geographical locations. Mises dislikes all such metaphorical terms which falsely imply a similarity between the automatic movements of mechanics and the individual choices involved in all human actions.

HA. 600.

Unemployment, institutional. Unemployment due to interferences with free market conditions rather than the voluntary decisions of those unemployed. Such interferences include all attempts to raise wage rates above the flexible rates which in a free market tend to adjust the supply of every type of labor to the demand for it. Such interferences are usually the result of so-called "pro-labor" legislation, although they may also be the result of custom, union activity or fear of violence.

HA. 600, 615, 769-779, 789-793; OG. 105; PF. 10-14; also PLG. 120-139, 239-246.

Unemployment, technological. Unemployment erroneously attributed to the introduction of improved methods of production, such as the use of more efficient capital equipment (tools, machinery, "automation," etc.). As long as unused, or not fully utilized, natural resources exist, there are always opportunities for additional employment in an unhampered market economy.

HA. 136-137, 774.

Unfavorable balance of payments. See "Balance of payments."

Unhampered market economy. See "Market economy, the free or unhampered."

Unio mystica, (Latin). Literally, unity or union by secret rites. More generally, the unity or union in the spirit of an individual with that of the Supreme Being or some other superior or leader.

Union, Unionists. Names given to the Northern States of the United States, and to their soldiers and citizens during the Civil War (q.v.).

United Nations. An international association of the governments of member nations (1945-   ), successor to the League of Nations (q.v.). Proposed early in World War II, the UN's Charter was drafted and went into force in 1945. Headquarters were later established in New York City. It consists of the Security Council with five permanent and ten elected members, the General Assembly with equal representation for each of its 135 member governments (as of September 18, 1973), the International Court of Justice with fifteen members, a Secretariat and a growing number of subsidiary specialized agencies, most of which have been organized for the promotion of specific types of interventionism among the member nations. UN actions and debates have indicated that its nationalist-minded members are almost unanimously imbued with the ideology that peace and economic progress can best be attained by policies of political interventionism rather than liberalism (see "Liberal").
   HA. 368, 686-688, 825.

Universalism. A holistic or collectivist concept that considers a society as an acting entity with its own will and ends which are independent and separate from those of its individual members. The ends of the group are determined by a superhuman power and revealed through a leader whose authority and statements of "truth" can never be questioned by reason or faithful believers. Holding that families and communities direct the development of individuals, rather than vice versa, universalists consider social aggregates, such as nations, as an articulated whole to which the functions of individuals must be subordinated. Society's desired

143

ends are realized solely by compelling individuals to function as prescribed by the political community. A modern proponent of universalism was Othmar Spann (1878-1950) whose ideas formed the basis for much of Nazism.

EP. 43, 47-48, 153, 209-210; HA. 44-45, 145-153.

Uno acto, (Latin). By a single doing; with one action.

Unpropitious. The opposite of propitious (q.v.).

Usufruct. The right to use and enjoy the property of another to the extent that such use and enjoyment does not destroy or diminish its essential substance.

Usurers. Lenders of money at interest, carrying the implication that such lenders charge an exorbitant, or excessively high, interest rate.

Utilitarianism. A school of thought, neutral as to ends, that holds that social cooperation, ethical precepts and governments are, or should be, merely useful means for helping the immense majority attain their chosen ends. It holds that the ultimate standard of good or bad as to means is the desirability or undesirability of their effects. It rejects the notions of human equality, of natural law, of government as an instrument to enforce the laws of God or Destiny; and of any social entity, such as society or the State, as an ultimate end. It recommends popular government, private property, tolerance, freedom and equality under law not because they are natural or just but because they are beneficial to the general welfare.

HA. 148, 175-176; OG. 50-51; TH. 49, 55-61.

Utopia. An utterly impractical plan or scheme for an ideal human existence which is unattainable because of the inherent character of man. Utopians are impractical idealists or dreamers removed from reality.

Utopians, socialist. See "Socialism, scientific and utopian."

V

Value (i.e., Subjective economic value as contrasted with objective use-value, q.v.). The importance that acting man attaches to ultimate ends. Means (factors of production, q.v.) acquire value as man ascribes to them a usefulness in facilitating the attainment of an ultimate end. Value is not intrinsic; it is not in things. It is within the human mind; it reflects the way in which man reacts emotionally to the conditions of his environment. Value is reflected in human conduct. It is not what a man or groups of men say about value that counts, but how they act. Value is always relative, subjective and human, never absolute, objective or divine. See "Marginal theory of value" and "Subjective-value theory."

B. 27; HA. 96; TH. 19-69; UF. 37; also PLG. 27-54.

Value judgments. See "Judgment of value."

Vandals. A group of Teutonic (German) tribes, who, during the fifth century, fought their way westward across the Rhine (406) and the Pyrenees (409). Led by their hero king, Genseric (d.477), from 428 to 477, they went on to Africa where they captured Carthage (439) and made it their capital. From this base, they attacked Constantinople and Rome, plundering and destroying all in their way. With Genseric's death, their power declined rapidly.

Although the Vandals were probably no worse than their contemporaries, their name has become a synonym for wanton and willful destroyers of the property of others, particularly works of art.

Vassal. A feudal tenant who, in return for military service or its equivalent, occupies and manages a feudal estate or fief at the pleasure of a superior lord, king or emperor. See "Feudalism."

Verstehen, (German). Understanding. See definition of "Understanding."

Vested interests. Established or entrenched positions; existing claims, right or privileges.

Vicissitudes. Rapid, unpredictable and often violent changes which completely alter the previously existing situation.

Vikings. Scandinavian seafaring adventurers who, starting about 788, ravaged European coastlands for two centuries. Operating from seaport bases they repeatedly raided the countryside before being gradually absorbed in the local populations. They originally plundered and finally settled along the coastal areas of what are now Germany, the Netherlands, England, France, Eire, Spain, Portugal and along the western and northern shores of the Mediterranean as far east as northern Italy.

OG. 135-136.

Volkswirtschaft -en, n., *volkswirtschaftlich -e,* adj., (German). National political economy in the sense of a nation's politically directed or controlled economy or even national socialism. The term implies that the welfare or interests of the nation or society are somehow different from, superior to, and often opposed to those of the nation's individual inhabitants.

HA. 323-326, 399, 516, 521.

Volonté générale, (French). General will.

Vorlesungen zur Phänomenologie des inneren Zeitbewusstseins, (German). Lectures on the inner (mental) consciousness of time.

W

Weber-Fechner law.   Ernst H. Weber (1795-1878) proclaimed his law of psycho-physics that the least noticeable increase in the intensity of a human sensation is always brought about by a constant proportional increase in the previous stimulus. Gustav T. Fechner (1801-1887) developed this into the Weber-Fechner law that to increase the intensity of a sensation in arithmetical progression, it is necessary to increase the intensity of the stimulus in geometric progression.

Wehrwirtschaftslehre, (German).   The teaching of the economics of war or defense, or the economics of military weapons and supplies.

Welfare principle, welfare economics.   The popular theory of a group, sometimes called the welfare school, who believe they can improve capitalistic conditions by interventions which they claim will reduce poverty, economic insecurity and inequalities in income and wealth. Their policies are inconsistent with their aims in that they seek higher living standards for the masses while advocating policies which grant special privileges that tend to reduce human incentives and capital accumulation, without which higher productivity and living standards become impossible.

AC. 111; B. 42; HA. 833-854.

Weltgeist, (German).   World spirit or intellect.

Wertfrei, adj. *Wertfreiheit,* n., (German).   Literally, "value free" and "value freedom." Actually, neutral with regard to all judgments of value (q.v.). All sciences, including economics, are *wertfrei.*

EP. 35-37, 57; HA. 47-48.

Wirtschaftliche Staatswissenschaften, (German).   The economic aspects of political science.
   B. 83; HA. 62, 605, 761-762.

Wotan.   Also Woden and Odin. The god of war and wisdom.

Z

Zadruga, (Serbian). A rural community composed of a large family of from 15 to 70 related adult Slavs and their children. The members ate, lived and worked in communal family style. The house father and house mother assigned the tasks and apportioned rights according to each individual relationship to the founder. The house father occupied the hamlet's best and largest house with the common kitchen, dining and living rooms. The other houses were primarily crude sleeping quarters. The main occupations were farming, grazing and tending orchards and vineyards. No property could be sold except by common consent. In ancient times, *Zadrugas* were fairly common in the rural and mountain areas of what is now Yugoslavia and Bulgaria and a few of them continued down to recent years.

Zeus. The chief of the pantheon of the Greeks and the Greek counterpart of the Roman god, Jupiter, at about 1000 B.C. He was worshipped as the omnipresent, all powerful Father or Master of all Gods.

Zwangswirtschaft, (German). An economic system entirely subject to government control. "*Zwang* means compulsion, *Wirtschaft* means economy. The English language equivalent for *Zwangswirtschaft* is something like compulsory economy." (*Socialism,* p. 529n.)

B. 65; HA. 764; OG. 56-58, 179n, 203-206, 225; PF. 24, 77; S. 529, 533, 584.

APPENDIX A

A CRITIQUE OF
BÖHM-BAWERK'S REASONING
IN SUPPORT OF
HIS TIME PREFERENCE THEORY

by

Ludwig von Mises

This is the critical analysis to which Mises refers in Human Action, *3rd ed. page 488, note 5 (Chicago: Regnery, 1966); 1st ed., page 485, note 5 (New Haven: Yale, 1949). It appeared in* Nationalökonomie *(Geneva, Switzerland: Editions Union, 1940), pp. 439-444. This excerpt has been translated from the German by Bettina Bien Greaves and edited by Percy L. Greaves, Jr.*

In order to appreciate this critique, it is important to realize that, while Mises gave Böhm-Bawerk full credit for his important analysis of the phenomenon of interest, he pointed out here that Böhm-Bawerk failed to understand why *present goods regularly attain a higher value than physically identical future goods do, i.e., the sole cause giving rise to the phenomenon of interest. Mises went on to explain in* Nationalökonomie, *as he does in Chapter XVIII of* Human Action *(1949/ 1963/1966), that time preference is an inherent category of human action. For the same reason that "a bird in the hand is worth two in the bush," present goods are worth more than the identical items in an uncertain future. Present goods are more valuable than future goods not because of some psychological factor or personal value judgment of particular persons at particular times and places—but simply because the present goods are available here and now and the future goods are not. Thus, interest is a praxeological consequence of man's cognition of time. Individuals are bound—by the limitations of the universe and the very nature of man with his a priori or innate awareness of time— to place a lower value on future goods than they do on present goods. However, to call this* lower *valuation an UNDER-valuation, as Böhm-Bawerk did, is a judgment of value and not a scientific statement.*

BBG & PLG.

Böhm's Theory Based on Psychology

In his trail-blazing inquiry into the problem of interest, Böhm-Bawerk starts with the assertion that present goods are in every in-

150

stance more valuable than future goods of the same kind and quantity.*
He then attempts in two different ways to prove this theory on psychological grounds.

The second reason** offered by Böhm-Bawerk for the higher valuation of present goods as compared with future goods is that future needs and the means available for satisfying them are regularly, but incorrectly, *under*-valued (i.e., valued too low). Böhm holds that there can be no doubt that this under-valuation exists. He attributes this to (1) lack of knowledge about our future needs, (2) indecision which, among other things, leads us to prefer present enjoyment to future enjoyment even when we know this choice is not in our overall welfare, and finally (3) the realization that life is both short and uncertain. All these factors operate in this direction.

These psychological factors, to which Böhm-Bawerk looks for an explanation of the *under*-valuation of future requirements, undoubtedly do exist. Moreover, they certainly can affect human actions. They certainly play an important role in the decisions of many persons. Still— and Böhm-Bawerk recognized this—they affect different individuals to a very different extent and they affect the same individuals differently at different times when they are in different moods and humors. Böhm-Bawerk also noted that a tendency to *over*-value future goods may appear among those person who have fanatical fears for the future.

In discussing such psychological factors, we should keep in mind that they are not inexorably and universally true. We may assume, if we wish, that many men are regularly driven by the factors cited by Böhm-Bawerk to *under*-value future needs. But then we must also consider the effect of antithetical psychological factors which lead some to place *higher* valuations on future goods. We may, if we choose, disregard those persons who might be considered mentally disturbed— misers and those with a fanatical fear of not having enough in the future. But then we must also disregard the opposite pathological types who give no thought at all to the future—the wild spenders, the simpletons too dull to conceive of any future worries and those who are depressed by the fear of some serious and imminent danger.

---

* See Böhm-Bawerk, Eugen. *Capital and Interest.* 3 volumes. English translation from the German 4th edition (South Holland, Ill.: Libertarian Press, 1959). This section discussed here appears in Volume II, pp. 259ff. Page citations in this translation are to this edition and volume.

** Mises discusses Böhm-Bawerk's *first* reason below, immediately following this critique of his *second* reason. BBG.

Some Persons Sacrifice for the Future

Still, we cannot overlook the fact that a higher valuation of the future may also play an important role in some human actions. The following typical cases come to mind: (1) the young man who turns down immediate employment at a moderate income and chooses present privation while training for work which promises a higher income later; (2) the saver or purchaser of insurance who foregoes present spending for current satisfaction in order to provide funds for his own or his family's future satisfaction; (3) the man who prefers a lower-salaried position with pension benefits to a higher-salaried position without such future benefits; and (4) the entrepreneur who maintains a modest standard of living while plowing back a large part of his earnings into the business.

Capitalist savings and providing for the future through insurance are not always possible. Before there can be such savings, certain institutional conditions must exist. There must be established systems of banking, insurance, savings and loan organizations and, above all, a money free from inflationary influences. However, the fact that monetary savings cannot take place in the absence of such conditions, no more weakens the significance of these arguments concerning the reason for interest than does the fact that entrepreneurs and capitalists, threatened with expropriation, prefer to consume their capital rather than to surrender it to the expropriator. The truth is that wherever the institutional conditions necessary for financial savings have existed people have made ample use of them.

According to Böhm's second reason, people regularly prefer present goods to future goods because they (incorrectly) *under*-value *future* goods. Following this line of reasoning, one could say that the persons described in the examples cited above were (incorrectly) *under*-valuing *present* goods as against future goods, but that it is easy for them, after providing adequately for the present, to set aside something for the future which would otherwise be provided for less generously. However, there is no justification for this interpretation. Certainly this argument does not apply to the student preparing himself, at the cost of present self-denial, for a more lucrative future occupation. Nor does it apply to the young employee who works for a future pension, or to the other examples. None of these typical cases refers to persons who, in Böhm-Bawerk's words, "are excessively well provided for in the present, or at least would be if they wished to consume completely in the present all the means currently available to them." (II:442, note #23) Rather they are persons who purposely reduce

152

their present standard of living in order to provide for a better future. They do this despite the fact that—from the viewpoint of their own subjective values—it represents present self-denial and renunciation.

Capitalism Encourages Persons to Save

As mentioned above, one may understand these things only by referring to observations made where social conditions permit the accumulation of monetary savings to provide for the future. The capitalistic economic order, inspired by the spirit of liberalism,* created conditions which permitted the development of thrift and thus, for the first time, offered the masses a choice between satisfying chronologically more immediate or more distant needs. Before then, saving had been restricted to the relatively small ranks of entrepreneurs and owners of real estate. Therefore, the tremendous increase in capital formation under capitalism has been, to a considerable extent, the result of the saving of the masses. However, despite the fact that capitalism provided the masses with a substantial increase in well-being, it certainly cannot be said that they have been so "excessively well provided for" that they *under*-valued present goods and thus found saving for the future easy.

Saving would certainly have become a much more widespread practice, even a mass mania, if two influences had not operated in the opposite direction: (1) the increasing threat to capital accumulation as a result of anticapitalistic tendencies and (2) the systematic derision of the practice of saving and the undermining of the value of saving, which came with the spread of an anti-capitalistic ideology. Liberalism recommended saving to the person of modest means as the only way to improve his future situation. Socialistic propaganda strove to demonstrate the opposite, namely that saving could never make individuals prosperous. According to the socialistic doctrine, capital arises—not from saving—but from the accumulation of profits produced by the exploitation of foreign labor and by the appropriation of surplus labor value.

One could surely find support for asserting that it may be a characteristic of the capitalistic economy to *over*-value future needs, rather than to *under*-value them as Böhm claims. However, such statements always concern psychological situations which lack inexorability and universality. Some persons are motivated to varying degrees by ideas which lead them to *under*-value future needs and the means for satisfying them. Others, however, *over*-value future needs and the means for satisfying them. A *universal* phenomenon, such as the *higher* val-

---

* See "Liberal," sense (1), above pp. 79-80.

153

uation, as opposed to an *over*-valuation, of present goods and the *lower* valuation, as opposed to an *under*-valuation, of the same goods in the future can never be explained satisfactorily by the existence of psychological factors which affect different people differently.

Some Persons Expect a Brighter Future

Coming now to the *first reason* Böhm-Bawerk suggests for the higher valuation of present goods, namely that there are different ratios between want and provision at different periods of time. This attempt at an explanation is no more successful than his other. Here also the facts involved lack universality. Certainly, some persons endure privation in the present, hoping to be better provided for later. However, there are others, as Böhm also conceded, for whom the opposite holds true. In this latter category he included "a very considerable number of persons whose income is derived entirely, or in large part, from their personal activity and will therefore presumably cease in the later years of their lives when they become incapable of working." (II:266) In saying this, Böhm obviously intended to minimize the significance of the fact that these people were in a position to retain present goods for use in the future, using them in the meantime as a reserve fund. These people would then value present goods no less than future goods and perhaps even somewhat more. Only in a dwindling minority of cases, wherein special circumstances impede or threaten any transfer from the present to the future, will present goods possess for their owners a smaller subjective use value than future goods. In such situations—even if there is no contributing influence other than the difference between supply and demand in present and future—the outcome of the subjective valuations which determine objective exchange values must obviously be such as to give present goods a powerful advantage, a considerable agio (premium) over future goods. (II:268)

Böhm-Bawerk did not recognize that the first reason he suggested for the greater valuation of present over future goods—that there are different ratios between demand and supply at different points in time —was rendered inconclusive by the fact that so many people actually *do* provide for the future, and not for the most immediate future only. The fact that the future is taken care of at all, the fact that present satisfaction actually *is* foregone to provide for the future, is proof that people expect that, in the absence of such precautions, the future would be inadequately provided for as compared with the present. It is irrelevant whether the number of persons who suffer want in the present while hoping to be more richly provisioned at a future time is larger or smaller. For, as Böhm realized, this group also divides into two sharply separated sub-groups:

(1) The first sub-group is made up of children and the sick, persons without present resources, for whom only the lapse of time can bring improvement. When they have grown, or are well once more, they will be able to work. In a society which lived from hand to mouth and, thus, was not familiar with credit transactions (the trading of present goods for future goods), such persons would be left to starve, unless protected by family loyalty or humanitarianism. However, in a society where provisions are being made for the future also, such persons, or their legal advisers or guardians acting on their behalf, can discount their future capacity to work and their anticipated future prosperity. In that way, today can be made more secure by reason of tomorrow's expectations. They can do this only because other people are so well provided for in the present that they may provide now for their future, a future which, in their opinion, would otherwise be under-provisioned. This is still clearer with respect to the other sub-group.

(2) The second sub-group is composed of those who—in Böhm-Bawerk's words—"look forward with confidence to a career that will bring economic improvement." (II:266) These persons are preparing themselves for a calling, or taking preliminary steps in a profession, which promises to be remunerative only after some time. Such persons, who do not themselves have the means necessary to carry on during the training or waiting period, may arrange for a more distant future in this way because *other* persons *do* have these means available. These other persons lend out some of their present resources precisely because they, the lenders, being *relatively* over-provisioned in the present, may thus better provide for their own security in the future.

Only Savers Provide Choices Between Present and Future Goods

Differing ratios of demand to supply at various periods of time can explain why transactions being undertaken now take into consideration both the present and the future. However, these different ratios cannot explain why future goods are regularly valued *lower* than present goods. In the hypothetical case that future goods were to be valued as high or higher than present goods, persons who were currently well provisioned would still, if they feared future deprivation, choose to set aside a part of their present goods for future needs. It is not surprising that persons who suffer want in the present, but hope to be better supplied in the future, are prepared to value present goods higher

155

than future goods. However, it is not they who play the decisive role on the market where present goods are exchanged against future goods. The significant role devolves on those who actually have at their disposal present goods, some of which they can decide to use for immediate satisfaction or for more distant future wants. It is they who choose between present and future goods. It is as a result of *their* choices that the differences in value appear which lead to the problem we are trying to explain.

All Consumers Prefer Present Goods

Böhm-Bawerk's error consisted primarily in the fact that he sought to base the theory of the higher valuation of present goods on psychological grounds. However, a universally true theory may never be attained via psychological paths. Psychology can show us that *some* persons, or even *many* persons, are guided by certain influences. But psychology can *never* demonstrate that a definite conduct is necessarily always and in the same way common to all men.

As a matter of fact, what Böhm-Bawerk actually succeeds in demonstrating is only that it appears plausible for men to place higher values on *present* goods than future goods under *some* circumstances, while under *other* circumstances it appears no less plausible for the opposite to be true, i.e., for *future* goods to be more highly valued than present goods. What Böhm-Bawerk's thesis comes down to then is that some types of persons are inclined toward an incorrect *under*valuation of future goods, while others lean toward an incorrect *over*valuation of future goods.

      ✶   ✶   ✶   ✶

Böhm-Bawerk therefore merely arrived at the conclusion that "as a rule" future goods have a lower value than the same kind and quantity of present goods. But that is not a satisfactory explanation. Are there exceptions to this rule? If there are, what significance do they have for explaining interest? Might the exceptions not become the rule under certain circumstances and interest then disappear entirely?

No, there are no such exceptions! In acting, one must always, without any exception, value a satisfaction at an earlier point in time more than the same kind and amount of satisfaction at a later time. If this were not so, then it would never be possible to decide in favor of a present satisfaction. Whoever uses or consumes anything, whoever seeks by acting to relieve to a greater or lesser extent a felt uneasiness is always expressing a preference for an earlier over a later satisfaction. Whoever eats and consumes anything is making a choice between a satisfaction in the immediate future and one in a more distant future. If he were to decide differently, if he were not to prefer the earlier to the later satisfaction, he would never be able to consume at all. He could not even eat and consume tomorrow, because when tomorrow became today, and the day after tomorrow became tomorrow, the decision to consume would still call for valuing an earlier satisfaction more than a later satisfaction. Otherwise, consumption would have to be delayed still further.

APPENDIX B

Economic calculation.   The process by which fallible men acting in a changing world choose among an infinite variety of imaginable and possible methods of production. In a market economy, prices stem from the bids and asks of producers and consumers. Thus, prices reflect the relative urgency of their various wants. The prices at which goods and services are traded influence the choices consumers and producers make when bidding for final products, natural resources, as well as produced and semi-produced factors of production. Higher (lower) prices reflect greater (lesser) demand and/or greater (lesser) scarcity of a good or service and induce users to conserve (splurge), and/or expand (contract) production. Thus market prices enable individuals—consumers and entrepreneurs—to calculate and to guide production so that the means available tend to be devoted to the most urgent wants, leaving no more urgently felt want unsatisfied. The two requisites for such a pricing system are (1) private ownership, not only of consumer's goods but also of factors of production, and (2) a common denominator, money, in which relative values may be expressed. Mises pointed out in 1920 that such calculations would be impossible in a socialist economy—*because the two conditions for economic calculation would be lacking.* Socialist planners would have to rely on outside prices to determine relative market values. This thesis evoked a lively, and ongoing, debate, as defenders of socialism attempted to refute Mises.

HA.200–231, 698–715; S.111–150. See Mises' 1920 essay and F. A. Hayek's contributions in *Collectivist Economic Planning* (Hayek, ed. Routledge & Kegan Paul, 1935). Also Don Lavoie's *Rivalry & Central Planning: The Socialist Calculation Debate Reconsidered* (Cambridge University Press, 1985).